THE
FUTURI

THE FUTURE

A GUIDE TO THE JEWISH MESSIAH, ISRAEL, AND THE END OF DAYS

RABBI LAWRENCE HAJIOFF

Distributed by:
Feldheim Publishers
POB 34549 / Jerusalem, Israel
208 Airport Executive Park
Nanuet, NY 10954
www.feldheim.com

This book is dedicated to the marriage
of Asher David Milstein to Michelle Tadmor.
May they build a beautiful Torah home together.

Rabbi S.F. Zimmerman
Rov of Gateshead

שרגא פייבל הלל זימערמאן
אבד דקק גייטסהעד

יום ד' לס' אמ"ו תשרו

My dear friend & colleague [& former student]
Rabbi Lawrence Hajioff has a unique talent of
being able to transmit our ancient Torah & Tradition
in contemporary terms to todays generation — He has
given lectures on the topic of the End of days over
a five year period — He has now collected these lectures
in a book called "The Future: The Jewish Messiah, Israel
& the End of Days" — I perused it & found it to be very
enlightening & to provide clarity about our uncertain times
we are living in — I highly recommend it for the advanced
scholar & novice student alike.

It is my blessing that Rabbi Hajioff should continue his holy
work in good health, peace of mind & naches from his family
& students

95 BEWICK ROAD, GATESHEAD, NE8 1RR
TEL: 0191 477 1847   FAX: 0191 477 7688

TABLE OF CONTENTS

ACKNOWLEDGMENTS

THIS BOOK IS dedicated to my good friend Asher David Milstein. Without him this book would never have become a reality. Not only did he contribute his resources, but he also gave me encouragement throughout the writing of the book. On one occasion, I became nervous at the thought of writing a book on such an important topic. I asked him if I should abandon the manuscript and write on a topic that was less serious in nature. Asher took me to task, telling me that writing a book on such a topic was needed in our generation and that plenty of other authors could tackle less important topics; "This book must be written!" Asher, your dedication to your people and Jewish scholarship is an inspiration to us all.

I am so glad Asher found and married his *eishes chayil*, Michelle. May Hashem grant you both many happy and healthy years together. Mazal Tov!

Thank you to my good friends and supporters Gabe and Yaara Plotkin. They are true givers and never ask anything in return. Their incredible love for the Land of Israel and for those who put their lives on the line protecting the Land is inspiring. May G-d bless them with continued health and happiness, and may they have much *nachas* from their beautiful children Eytan Shmerel, Carmel Clara, and Ori Arthur.

Ever since Emily and Arik Shteinhauz met on my Israel trip, they have been friends and supporters of all my projects. Thank you for your friendship, and may you have much pride from your children, Aaron, Adam, and Benjamin.

A big thank you to everyone at Mosaica Press. Rabbi Yaacov Haber and Rabbi Doron Kornbluth believed in this project and dedicated their wisdom and scholarship to help me bring this book to the market. I am so grateful to them and their incredible team.

My dear friends Moshe and Nomi Wiederman are wonderful supporters of my projects. Thank you, guys, and may you have much success and continued *nachas* from all your children.

Yehoshua and Nechama Nisenbaum have been constant supporters of all my projects. May Hashem bless them and their wonderful children with continued success in all their endeavors. They are models of what great Jewish parents can be.

A very big thank you to my dear friend Rabbi Immanuel Bernstein for reviewing the manuscript and offering his comments. He greatly enhanced the book.

Thank you to Estela Berry for sponsoring this book in honor of her children, Moises Egozi, Mario Egozi, and Devorah bas David, of blessed memory.

My parents, Rachel and Maurice Hajioff, raised me and my siblings with a great pride in our Judaism and a love for the Land of Israel. May Hashem grant them many more happy and healthy years together and may they have continued *nachas* from their children and grandchildren.

Finally, thank you to my dear wife, Anita. She put up with me secluding myself in my office for countless hours, which permitted me to write this book, while she tended to our home and children. May she be blessed with all good things.

INTRODUCTION

WHAT DOES THE future hold in store for mankind? What do all the events we see in the news really mean? These questions and many more like them are on many people's minds. Consider just a few challenges the world is facing:

- The proliferation of nuclear weapons around the world, many of which are in the hands of terrorist regimes
- The Middle East caught in frequent wars and seemingly on the edge
- Much of Western Europe cowering in fear as terrorist atrocities occur on a regular basis
- The rise of anti-Semitism the world over and the periodic attacks against the Jewish people in Israel, as well as the existential threat Israel faces from its closest neighbors

Is civilization crashing down on us, ready to return us to the Stone Age? Yet, at the same time, with all the fear of war, terrorism, death, and destruction paralyzing us, the world seems to be *progressing* at an incredible rate:

- Every day we hear of scientists discovering cures for diseases that have plagued mankind for centuries.
- Technology has opened up the world for us like never before, as people communicate at a speed and breadth never known before in world history.
- Most major international cities are building incredible skylines; people are traveling far and wide in record numbers; space travel is finally becoming a reality for the masses; and with all the

doomsayers predicting another financial meltdown around the corner, economies are continuing to grow ever bigger and robust with new technological products being available to more people than ever before.

Well, which is it? Is the world on the path to inevitable destruction, or are we progressing to something very new and great?

Amazingly, when we examine ancient Jewish sources, we can see that much of what is happening today has been foretold. Although there may be bumps along the road, the world is moving to a time of world peace, love, and redemption — for all its inhabitants. The time we are moving towards is called *Acharis HaYamim*, the End of Days. This phase of human existence is described in great detail in a myriad of Jewish sources. Let's examine what this time represents and how we are going to get there.

THE END OF DAYS

From the moment of Creation, when mankind began its journey through the millennia, everything that has happened — every nation created, every country conquered, every person born in every nation-state, all of it — has been leading us to this moment of world history. The Midrash explains that the coming of the Messiah, in Hebrew *Mashiach*, was actually put in place and prepared for at the beginning of Creation.[1] When the Torah says, "And the Spirit of G-d hovered over the surface of the water,"[2] the *Baal HaTurim* tells us that these words, "And the Spirit of G-d hovered," have the same *gematria*, numerical value, as the words, "this is the spirit of Mashiach." In other words, part of Creation itself was the creation of the future world where the Mashiach would be king.

---

1   *Bereishis Rabbah* 2:4.
2   *Bereishis* 1:2.

As we said, this time period is called in the Torah *Acharis HaYamim*, the End of Days.[3] Don't let that expression fool you. The expression "the End of Days" doesn't mean everything mankind has worked for up to this point will return to dust and rubble. On the contrary, it means that we have reached a point of history where mankind cannot continue as it has been and events need to happen that will clear the way for a new beginning that will far surpass everything the world has become accustomed to until now. In other words, it will be the end of the days that we have been accustomed to and the beginning of days that will be wholly different. It will be a time of sublime existence — one that we can only have dreamed about.

This entire redemptive process has been foretold by the Jewish prophets in Scriptures and examined by countless Jewish scholars over the thousands of years of Jewish history. All of them spoke of these times that we are living in now with the most astonishing descriptions, which only those who live through these times can truly appreciate. We will witness miracles that haven't been experienced since the Exodus of the Jewish people from the Land of Egypt nearly three and a half thousand years ago, which we relive each year at the Passover Seder. So incredible will these days be that they will surpass the miracles that happened during the Exodus from Egypt.

All of these world events we are told will center around the Middle East and particularly the holy city of Yerushalayim, the eternal capital of Israel and the Jewish people. It is not a coincidence that if you open the newspapers and news sites today many of the stories revolve around the events happening in the Middle East right now.

According to the Jewish Scriptures, all of these world events (especially those happening in and around Israel) are preparing the world for the ultimate Redemption of mankind, which according to the Rambam is a basic principle of faith in Jewish thought.[4] The ultimate crowning

---

3   *Devarim* 4:30.

4   Rambam's commentary to the Mishnah, *Sanhedrin*, Thirteen Principles of Jewish Faith, principle twelve.

moment of everything that has happened and is happening now is leading us to the return of monarchy in the Land of Israel, which will be led by the Mashiach. The Mashiach — a human being of flesh and blood — will lead a spiritual revolution where peace will reign for all the people in the world so that we can all start a new beginning of love, peace, and true world harmony.

CAN IT REALLY BE CALLED THE END OF DAYS?

The better translation of *Acharis HaYamim* is "in the days to come." The expression "End of Days" implies that time itself will come to an end upon the arrival of the Mashiach. Nothing could be further from the truth. The term "End of Days," however, may actually work well if you understand them to mean the "end result." This means that the culmination of all of world history will be flowing towards that point of time. It will be the end of our final exile, and all of the troubles of the Jewish people will finally come to an end.

So the expression *Acharis HaYamim*, the End of Days, is not the end of days as the destruction of the world, but as Rabbi Samson Raphael Hirsch writes, "It is the end result, the culmination of the legacy of days. It is the culmination of all of world history, which has been flowing towards that point."[5]

A NEW WORLD

Many of us were taught as children that in the Messianic era the world will continue to exist as it is today, though with a few minor improvements, such as world peace and the centrality of the Land of Israel for the Jewish people. However, the Maharal of Prague writes that such a superficial understanding doesn't give an appreciation to the real change the world will go through in the times of the Mashiach. So incredible will the change be that in reality the world will go through a completely new Creation in comparison to the world we have today. The world will be a spiritual world of true reality.[6]

---

5   Rabbi Samson Raphael Hirsch, *Bereishis* 49:1.
6   Maharal, *Netzach Yisrael* 47.

David HaMelech hinted to this new world in *Sefer Tehillim* when he says, "When G-d returns us to Zion, it will feel like we were dreamers."[7] The commentators explain this to mean that when the Mashiach comes, we will experience the world in such a completely different way that it will feel like we were waking up from a dream.[8] The spiritual world will feel palpable, and everything we have experienced in the Present World will seem like the stuff of dreams. It will be a complete awakening for all of humanity.

Why does the world need to change so much? Why is our world the way it is now?

Before we look at the Mashiach and examine his role, we have to step back into the Garden of Eden. G-d created this world with the end in mind. That means from the very beginning of the Creation of the Present World, the seeds of the Final Redemption were already planted. Let's begin with Adam and Chava and figure out how we got here in the first place.

---

7   *Tehillim* 126:1.
8   *Machashavos Charutz* 3.

Chapter One

ADAM AND CHAVA — BEGINNINGS IN GAN EDEN

THE TORAH TELLS us that G-d created heaven and earth.[9] After creating the world (with all of its trees, plants, oceans), He created mankind in the form of Adam and Chava.

Adam and Chava were the last part of G-d's Creation and were created with two opposites:

- a pure spiritual soul
- an unenlightened physical body

The body and soul are both drawn towards their nature:

- the soul leans towards the spiritual
- the body inclines towards the material

The body and soul are in a constant state of battle. The body wishes to pursue physical desires, food, drink, and bodily desires. The soul wants more spiritual and meaningful experiences that connect it to the spiritual world, such as performing acts of kindness, prayer, and goodness.

When Adam and Chava were first formed, they too had two equal opposites, the body and soul, and they had free will to choose between doing acts of good and of evil.

---

9   *Bereishis* 2:15.

G-d placed Adam and Chava in the Garden of Eden to work it and to eat freely of its fruits. This, say the commentators, was metaphorical, because the Garden itself was plentiful and didn't need work done to it at all.[10] Everything Adam (and eventually Chava) needed was already there in the Garden, ready for them to enjoy. All Adam and Chava needed to do was be involved in spiritual pursuits and to enjoy the beautiful world G-d had given them.

They were given two commands in relation to the Garden:

- First, they should enjoy all the fruit that was in the Garden.
- Second, they were not to eat from the "Tree of Knowledge of Good and Bad." They were warned, "For on the day you eat of it, you shall surely die." This means that death was not part of Creation at this point; however, by eating from the tree, evil impulses of jealousy, lust, and honor would be aroused inside them, making it impossible to attain the goal of complete spirituality as long as they were on earth. So eternal life would have been an intolerable burden for them.

Within a short amount of time, a serpent came to persuade Chava to eat from the tree. This was, however, not any ordinary serpent; it represented the evil inclination. Using its impressive power of persuasion, the serpent encouraged Chava to eat from the one tree that was forbidden to her. She ate and then gave Adam to eat as well. One of the commandments that they were given was transgressed — and the course of history would change forever.

> What would the world have looked like had Adam and Chava not sinned?

ADAM AND CHAVA AFTER THE SIN

What would the world have looked like had Adam and Chava not sinned?

We don't know the answer to that question, but we *do* know that had they not sinned, Adam and Chava would have been able to attain spiritual greatness for the body as well as the soul.

---

10   *Pirkei D'Rebbi Eliezer, Bereishis* 2:15.

When they sinned, everything changed. The amount of evil that existed initially was just enough to allow Adam and Chava to gain spiritual perfection through their own efforts. After their sin, evil increased in the world and it became much harder to achieve good in this world. The evil inclination was no longer an external reality (as it appeared in the serpent), but entered inside Adam and Chava and concealed itself. It became much more challenging to discern good from evil in the world.[11]

Not only did it become difficult to know the difference between good and evil, it also required much more effort to abandon evil. Adam and Chava could no longer earn perfection as easily as before they sinned. The effort required to earn perfection now became a double task:[12]

- Mankind has to first bring itself to perfection.
- The world itself must return to the state it existed in before the first sin.

All of world history is really the return of mankind to the original state of Adam and Chava before the sin. This will only be finally reached when the Mashiach comes and returns the world to that original state. Unlike the original Garden of Eden, now we need to earn perfection through our own efforts, rather than being created in a perfect world that requires no effort on our part.

Some questions remain: How much effort do we need to bring perfection to the world? When will the benefits of all this effort be (finally) experienced?

TWO WORLDS CREATED

The first letter of the Torah is the second letter of the Hebrew alphabet, the letter *Beis*. The commentators ask why G-d didn't begin the Torah with the first letter, *Aleph*. Among the many answers to this question is that G-d began the Torah with the second letter in order to allude to the number two. The number two reveals to us that G-d created *two*

---

11   *Nefesh HaChaim* 1:6.
12   *Derech Hashem*, part 1.

worlds at the beginning of Creation: *Olam Hazeh*, the Present World, and *Olam Haba*, the World to Come.

Why would G-d create two worlds? Isn't one sufficient?

Furthermore, what is the nature of these two worlds?

Rabbi Moshe Chaim Luzzato, in his work *Derech Hashem*, explains that G-d in His kindness did humanity a big favor: He limited the effort we need to expend in order to reach perfection. G-d therefore created two distinct periods: One period is a time for earning reward, and the other is a time for receiving reward.[13]

The general rule that G-d created the world with is that whatever pertains to good is always greater than that which pertains to evil. So the period of earning is limited and lasts no longer than G-d decreed suitable for this purpose. The period of reward on the other hand has no limit, and the enjoyment derived from reaching perfection lasts for all eternity.

Since the periods of earning reward and receiving reward are different, the environment each requires needs to be suitable for its role and, by definition, will be quite different from each other:

- While a person is striving for perfection, he must be in a setting containing all the necessary elements needed to obtain and reach that perfection. So the period of earning must therefore be one where maximum challenge exists and where the elements of physical and spiritual are in constant strife.
- In the period of reward, the exact opposite is true. The physical must be limited and the spiritual must be allowed to gain dominance. The soul must be allowed to blossom and the body must subdue itself to the soul's desires.

For this reason, G-d created two worlds called *Olam Hazeh* and *Olam Haba*, the Present World and the World to Come. Each world has all the necessary elements for mankind to do what is right in both worlds. The Present World is the world of work, challenge, and strife, and the World

---

13   Ibid. 1:3:2; translation by Rabbi Aryeh Kaplan (Feldheim Publishers), pgs. 45–47.

to Come is a world where all the fruits of our labors in the Present World will finally be realized.

One of the main highlights of the World to Come will be the revelation of the Mashiach. Let us understand who this person is and what his role in the End of Days will be all about.

Chapter Two

LET'S MEET THE JEWISH MESSIAH — MASHIACH

PEOPLE USUALLY TRANSLATE the Hebrew word for Messiah, *Mashiach*, as "savior."

This is not an accurate translation. While it is true that the Mashiach will have an epic task to fulfill for the Jewish people and the world, his task will be much greater than just "saving" people. If we examine the Hebrew term *Mashiach*, we will get a much better picture of his mission in this world. The word *Mashiach* actually means "the anointed one." Who is anointing him — and why?

KING OF ISRAEL

To become a king of the Jewish people and Israel, a prophet was required to anoint the soon-to-be-king with oil. He would do so by pouring the oil over the head of the future king. Using oil, which naturally rises to the top of water, he demonstrated to the Jewish people that this man was G-d's chosen to be king and rule over them.

Asking for a Jewish king is one of the 613 commandments. The Torah tells us, "When you come to the Land the Lord, your G-d, is giving you, and you possess it and live there, and you say, 'I will set a king over myself, like all the nations around me,' you shall set a king over you, one whom the Lord, your G-d, chooses; from among your brothers, you shall set a king over yourself; you shall not appoint a foreigner over yourself, one who is not your brother."[14]

This request for a king did not occur until the latter days of the life of Shmuel HaNavi when the people approached Shmuel and made the following demand: "You have grown old, and your sons did not follow in your ways, so now appoint a king to judge us, like all the other nations."[15] Even though the reasons for their request were far from ideal — "so we can be like the other nations" — rather than asking for a leader who could guide them to reach spiritual greatness, the prophet and G-d heeded their request. G-d told Shmuel, "Listen to their voice and crown a king for them."[16]

G-d granted them a man from the tribe of Binyamin as the first-ever king of the Jewish people. His name was Shaul and he was an outstanding choice: tall, distinguished, learned in Torah, G-d-fearing, and extremely humble. We will see that these and other traits are very important to successfully take on the mantle of king of the Jewish people.

When describing himself and his appointed position as a prophet of G-d, Yeshayah says, "The spirit of the Lord/*Elokim* is upon me, because G-d has anointed me to bring tidings to the humbled…"[17] Rashi explains that the word *lamashcha*, anointed, is an expression of leadership and greatness.[18] Although Yeshayah's use of this term is borrowed, still we can see that the word *Mashiach* is an expression of great leadership.

And that's exactly what "the Mashiach" will be — a leader of great distinction of the Jewish people and ultimately the entire world. Even our forefathers anticipated the eventual coming of the Mashiach. Let's see Avraham's role in bringing the Mashiach and the final redemption of the Jewish people.

---

14   *Devarim* 17:14–15.
15   *Shmuel I* 8:4.
16   *Shmuel I* 8:22.
17   *Yeshayah* 61:1.
18   Rashi, *Bamidbar* 18:8.

AVRAHAM PRAYS FOR THE MASHIACH

We see the great love Avraham had for all people, even the most wicked, during the episode of Sodom.

G-d had decided that because of their great cruelty to one another, the people of Sodom had lost their right to live. The Torah tells us, "So Hashem said, 'Because the outcry of Sodom and Gomorrah has become great and because their sin has been very grave, I will descend and see: If they act in accordance with its outcry that has come to Me, then destruction! And if not, I will know.'"[19]

Not wanting to keep this information from Avraham (especially as G-d had changed his name from Avram to Avraham, indicating his new role as father of the multitudes of nations), G-d said, "Shall I conceal from Avraham what I do?"[20]

Avraham took it upon himself to petition G-d on behalf of the people of Sodom and Gomorrah in order to save them. "What if there should be fifty righteous people in the midst of the city?" he inquired of G-d. "Would You still stamp it out rather than spare the place for the sake of the fifty righteous people? It would be sacrilege for You to do such a thing, to bring death on the righteous together with the wicked."[21]

When fifty righteous people could not be found, Avraham petitioned G-d to save the cities on behalf of forty-five righteous, then forty, then thirty, then twenty, and finally ten. Avraham did not give up. However, even ten righteous people could not be found and the decree of destruction was finalized.

On the surface, it seems as though Avraham's prayer failed because the cities were destroyed: "And so it was when G-d destroyed the cities of the plain that G-d remembered Avraham."[22]

However, consider the last few words mentioned: If G-d destroyed all the cities, in what way had he "remembered" Avraham?

---

19   *Bereishis* 18:20–21.

20   Ibid. v. 17.

21   Ibid. v. 24–25.

22   Ibid. 19:29.

The answer is given at the end of the same verse, "so He sent Lot from amidst the upheaval when he overturned the cities in which Lot had lived." Lot was Avraham's nephew who had grown up with him, but had decided to leave the spiritual benefit of living at Avraham's side and to move to Sodom.

When Avraham saw the destruction, he must have been heartbroken that his prayers had not been heard, but in actual fact they *had* been.

> Avraham's prayers about Sodom… were heard!

In the merit of Avraham's prayer, G-d had saved Lot and his two daughters. These daughters eventually started families of their own, which became the nations Amon and Moav. Many years later, a great descendant of Moav would exist by the name of Rus. Rus would become a righteous convert to Judaism and become the ancestor of David HaMelech himself. This means that the prayer of Avraham began the catalyst of events that would lead to David HaMelech and eventually the Mashiach himself! As the Midrash questions the verse in *Tehillim*, "'I found David my servant!'[23] Where was he found? In Sodom."[24]

The Midrash refers to this when describing the verse in the Torah, "Also Lot who went with Abram had flocks, cattle, and tents,"[25] whereupon the Midrash asks, "What were these tents? They refer to the Houses of Rus the Moabite and Naamah the Amonite."[26]

So Avraham's prayer for Sodom may have seemed like it had been for naught, yet from it came the roots of salvation that ended with the creation of David and eventually the Mashiach.

Rus the Moabite is key to this story. Let's examine how she merited being the mother of Jewish royalty.

---

23   *Tehillim* 89.
24   *Bereishis Rabbah* 50.
25   *Bereishis* 13:5.
26   *Bereishis Rabbah* 41:4.

THE MOTHER OF ROYALTY — RUS THE MOABITE CONVERT

One of the most fascinating episodes in Jewish history that is deeply connected to the future Mashiach is the story of Rus the Moabite. Rus was a non-Jewish Moabite princess, the daughter of King Eglon, who rose from non-Jewish royalty to become the great-grandmother of David HaMelech and thereby the great ancestress of the Mashiach himself.

How did she merit such an incredible role?

Before Israel had its first king, the nation was led by the Judges. This was a period that lasted from the death of Yehoshua and extended until Shaul HaMelech introduced monarchy to the Land of Israel, approximately a span of 350 years. During that time, there lived a Moabite princess named Rus who lived outside of Israel. A terrible famine had ravaged the Land of Israel, and a prestigious and wealthy family from Beis Lechem left Israel to find refuge in Moav. Their names were Elimelech, his wife Naomi, and their two sons, Machlon and Kilion.

Not too long after their arrival, Elimelech died an untimely death. Soon afterwards, his two sons married two Moabite women, Orpah and Rus. After a number of years Machlon and Kilion died too, so now only Naomi was left with her two daughters-in-law.

With the loss of her husband and two sons, Naomi was poor and broken. She decided that it was time to return to Israel. She turned to her two daughters-in-law and bid them farewell, instructing them to return to their families, "Go, return each of you to her mother's house. May G-d deal kindly with you as you have dealt kindly with the dead and with me!"[27]

Rus Refuses to Leave Naomi's Side

It was a very emotional farewell and they all cried bitterly. Orpah kissed her mother-in-law and returned to her family, but Rus clung onto Naomi, refusing to leave. Naomi tried to dissuade her from staying, "Look, your sister-in-law has returned to her people and to her god, go follow your sister-in-law." Rus, however, did not wish to leave

---

27   *Rus* 1:9.

but wanted to remain with Naomi and to become a full-fledged part of Naomi's people.

Rus then spoke the following beautiful words that have become the rallying cry of converts to Judaism for thousands of years: "Do not urge me to leave you, to turn back and not follow you. For wherever you go, I will go; where you live, I shall live, your people are my people, your G-d is my G-d, where you die, I will die, and there I will be buried."[28] And with that powerful statement of allegiance to Naomi, to G-d, and to the Jewish people, Rus, once the Moabite princess, became the prototype sincere convert to Judaism.

Naomi and Rus Arrive in Beis Lechem

People in Israel were shocked to see Naomi after all these years, especially in such a dejected and broken state. She had left Israel a wealthy woman and had returned a shadow of her previous self. Naomi's husband, Elimelech, had a nephew who was a very great man and a judge in Israel who was also very wealthy. His name was Boaz. Naomi and Rus arrived at one of his fields to glean some of the leftover stalks of wheat that the Torah commands field owners to leave for the poor and desolate people in Israel.

Boaz noticed the incredible way Rus acted in his fields — how she acted towards the people around her, how she took the exact amount of leftover stalks and not a single stalk more for fear of stealing from Boaz the owner of the field, and how Rus carried herself in a modest manner in dress and speech. In short, he was amazed by her and inquired into who she was. Upon finding out that Naomi was a relative of his, Boaz took extra care to look after her and her daughter-in-law without compromising an iota of her dignity.

Since Boaz's wife had died, Naomi decided that Rus would be an excellent match for him. Eventually Rus did end up marrying Boaz, as the Book of Rus tells us, "And so Boaz took Rus and she became his wife, and he came to her. G-d let her conceive and she bore a son."[29]

---

28   Ibid. v. 16–18.
29   Ibid. 4:13.

Upon seeing the child, the many women who had heard about this incredible union and extraordinary turn of events decided his name should be Oved, meaning "to serve," as a blessing that this child should serve G-d with a full heart.

The Book of Rus concludes with the following words: "Boaz had a son Oved, Oved had a son Jesse, Jesse had a son David." This is the clincher to the entire story: Rus the Moabite convert's devotion and selfless actions led her to become the great-grandmother of David HaMelech.

Rus ended up being blessed with a very long life and was able to see many descendants, even witnessing Shlomo HaMelech on his throne!

THE SURPRISING ORIGINS OF THE MASHIACH

It would be easy to assume that the Mashiach will come only from the most illustrious stock. He must be from a family of great and learned people who only acted with the greatest moral fortitude and ethical behavior. However, this is not completely true. While we know that the eventual Mashiach will be an incredibly spiritual and moral human being, what stands out in this story of Rus and the other stories of the Mashiach's ancestors is the lineage of the Mashiach and the unorthodox ancestry of the redeemer who comes to save his people.

It is actually quite astounding that the conception of the Davidic dynasty seems to be shrouded in so much impropriety. It began with Lot and his daughters who were miraculously saved from the destruction of Sodom. Thinking they were the only people left on earth, his daughters got him drunk, cohabited with him, and gave birth to Amon and Moav. Centuries later, Rus came from this nation Moav. Not exactly impressive lineage!

G-d had decided that the Mashiach should come from the seed of Rus, a convert. According to the *Akeidas Yitzchak*, this must have happened for a particular reason: "At the same time it also explains how two pearls in Jewish history, Rus and Naamah (a wife to Shlomo HaMelech and mother to his successor Rachavam) respectively came out of those two nations (Rus from Moav and Naamah from Ammon) and made their magnificent contribution to Jewish history by becoming ancestors of the ultimate redeemer, the Mashiach, so that David HaMelech had blood from those nations flowing in his veins."[30] Any good that was to come from those two nations will be part of the Mashiach and will enable him to fulfill his ultimate mission.

THE ANOINTING OIL OF MOSHE RABBEINU

As mentioned, part of the process of installing and coronating the new king was to anoint him by pouring oil on his head. Incredibly, Moshe Rabbeinu had been commanded to compound a special mixture of oil and spices, which was used to anoint and consecrate the Tabernacle, its vessels, and the Kohanim priests.[31]

> This oil was prepared in the time of Moshe Rabbeinu — hundreds of years before the first king.

Many years later, Shaul HaMelech made a terrible choice in judgment concerning Agag, the king of Amalek, by permitting him one last night of life when Shaul should have immediately killed him. (We'll be hearing much more about Amalek and their role in the End of Days later on.)

Because of this misjudgment, G-d decided that Shaul had forfeited his right to be king. Another man, this time from the tribe of Yehudah, was anointed king over Israel, whose name was David. As G-d told the prophet Shmuel, "How long will you mourn over Shaul when I rejected him from reigning over Israel? Fill your horn with oil and go forth, I shall send you to Jesse the Beis Lechemite, for I have seen a king for Myself among his sons."[32]

Appointing David as Shaul's successor was a major departure. David was the youngest of his siblings and a shepherd by trade. Furthermore, Shaul had been from the tribe of Binyamin and, had he fulfilled his mission, monarchy would have remained within his tribe forever. David was from the tribe of Yehudah. By switching to him, G-d had decided that from then

---

30   *Bereishis* 13:5.
31   *Shemos* 30:22–23.
32   *Shmuel I* 16:1.

on all kings until the Mashiach himself would be exclusively from the tribe of Yehudah and be direct descendants of David HaMelech as well.

A hint to the temporary nature of Shaul's kingship can be seen in the vessel choice used to anoint Shaul and David:[33]

- For Shaul's coronation, Shmuel used a flask — an ordinary vessel that eventually succumbs to the forces of nature.
- David, however, was anointed from a ram's horn, something that has the connotation of strength and constant power. And so Shmuel poured the oil onto David's head from a horn, demonstrating his tribe's kingship until the End of Days.

Fascinatingly, this same oil of Moshe Rabbeinu remained intact and un-diminished — despite its repeated use — until the time of King Yoshiyahu, when the destruction of the First Temple in Yerushalayim was imminent.

Where is it now? Like the Ark of the Covenant, this oil was hidden and will remain so until the coming of the Mashiach, when the same oil will be used to anoint the Mashiach himself. In addition, the horn that was used to anoint David (and every subsequent king) was kept in the Tabernacle and Temple. The Tabernacle was hidden away, as was the horn and the oil it contained. But one day, we hope in the not-too distant future, it will be found and used to anoint the future king, Mashiach.[34]

THE SIX THOUSAND YEARS OF WORLD HISTORY

The Talmud makes the following statement about the length of world history:

"The world is destined to exist for six thousand years; the first two thousand were nothingness, the second two thousand years were of Torah, the final two thousand years are ready for the Days of Mashiach."[35]

> The world is destined to exist for six thousand years.

---

33   *Kerisus* 6a.
34   Radak, *Shmuel I* 16:1.
35   *Avodah Zarah* 9a.

Let's consider the chronology:

- The first two thousand years were the years that preceded the birth of Avraham. Before his arrival, idol worship had taken a firm grip on the world's inhabitants to such a degree that a simple belief in one G-d was seen as lunacy. At a very young age, Avraham started to contemplate the amazing world around him and began believing in One Ultimate G-d as Unity in the universe. This stage of world history, one devoid of knowledge of G-d and filled with ungodly idol worship, is called *tohu vavohu*, amazing nothingness.

- The second set of two thousand years are called the years of Torah, as the rise of Avraham and his G-dly teachings culminated with the giving of the Torah on Mount Sinai in the Jewish year 2448. From that point on the world was filled with knowledge of and fulfillment of Torah.

The last set of two thousand years is appropriate for the redemption of the world. After the fourth millennia, the Mashiach should have come and released Israel and the Jewish people from the domination of the nations.[36] We are relatively close to completing these last two thousand years. They are the years that are ripest for the coming of the Mashiach. It has been our lack of worthiness that has prevented the Mashiach coming in these final two thousand years.

We can see a hint to the world existing for a maximum of six thousand years from the first verse in the Torah. According to the Gaon of Vilna, the essence of the entire Torah can be found in the first book of the Torah, *Bereishis*. The first book can be found in the first Torah portion *Bereishis*, and the first Torah portion can be found in the first verse of the Bible.

The first verse tells us: "In the beginning of G-d's creating of the heavens and the earth." The Hebrew letter *Aleph* appears six times in this verse. As well as being the first Hebrew letter in the alphabet, the letter

---

36   Rashi, *Avodah Zarah* 9a.

Aleph with a slight vowel change also spells the word *eleph*, which means "a thousand." So, the appearance of six *Alephs* connotes six *elephs*, i.e., six thousand years. From the very moment of Creation, G-d hinted to us in His Torah that the world as we know it can only last a maximum of six thousand years.

THE RAMBAM'S THIRTEEN PRINCIPLES OF FAITH

The Rambam lists Thirteen Principles of Jewish Faith. (A full list of these principles and their explanation can be found at the end of this book.) According to the Rambam, these principles are so crucial to whom we are as a people that without believing in them, one has excluded himself from the Jewish people altogether. In the words of the Rambam: "When a person believes fully and genuinely in all the Thirteen Principles of Faith, that person is truly considered part of the Jewish people and it is obligatory to love him, to have mercy on him, and to relate to him according to all the mitzvos that G-d has commanded concerning interpersonal relationships of love and brotherhood, and he has a share in the World to Come."[37]

The Rambam goes even further in his explanation of the importance of believing in the Mashiach's arrival. He says:[38]

> *In the future, the Messianic King will arise and renew the Davidic dynasty, restoring it to its initial sovereignty. He will build the Temple and gather the dispersed of Israel. Then, in his days, the observance of all the statutes will return to their previous state. We will offer sacrifices, observe the Sabbatical and Jubilee years according to all their particulars as described by the Torah.*
>
> *Anyone who does not believe in him [the Mashiach] or does not await his arrival denies not only the statements of the other prophets, but those of the Torah and Moshe, our teacher. The*

---

37   Rambam, commentary on the Mishnah, *Sanhedrin* 10:1.
38   Rambam, *Mishneh Torah, Melachim* 11:1.

Torah testified to his coming when it says, "G-d will bring back your captivity and have mercy upon you. He will again gather you from among the nations… Even if your dispersal is at the ends of the heavens, G-d will gather you up from there…and bring you to the Land."[39]

We shall see that based on the words of the Jewish prophets, the signs that were given to them have actually begun in full force and the impending redemption of the Jewish people, the Land of Israel, and the entire world is imminent.

THE SIX-FOLD MISSION OF THE MASHIACH

Let us explore (in detail!) the Mashiach's main mission. The prophets and Sages list six main missions that the Mashiach will need to accomplish, some of which he will do in order to prove that he indeed is the true Mashiach. Let's examine these six missions of the Mashiach:

Mission One: He will cause the world to return to G-d and His teachings.

This does not mean they will (or need to) become Jewish, although early on during the Messianic events they will have that opportunity to convert, as we'll see. However, no matter their race, culture, or religion, every human will fully accept the G-d of the Jewish people as the true G-d of all people.

Mission Two: He will restore the royal dynasty to the descendants of David HaMelech.

After many centuries of Jewish kings leading the Jewish people in Israel, exile led to the termination of Jewish kings. One of the key missions of the Jewish Mashiach will be the return of the monarchy to the Jewish people. The Mashiach will be the first of these kings and will continue in his bloodline to his children.

---

39   *Devarim 30:3–5.*

Mission Three: He will oversee the rebuilding of Yerushalayim, including the Third (and final) Temple in Yerushalayim.

The Mashiach will be tasked with rebuilding the Third and final Temple in Yerushalayim on the exact same spot as the first two Temples. As we will see, this knowledge of the exact location of the Temple will be revealed to the Mashiach through prophecy, as no mortal could ever exactly know where the various parts of the Temple should actually go without Divine help.

Mission Four: He will gather the Jewish people from all over the world to the Land of Israel.

For the past two thousand years, since the destruction of the Second Temple, the Jewish people have been scattered throughout the world. The prophets have reminded us that this dispersion is a temporary reality, and the Mashiach will be tasked with returning all the Jewish people to their ancestral homeland, the Land of Israel.

> Mashiach will be tasked with returning all the Jewish people to the Land of Israel.

Mission Five: He will reestablish the Sanhedrin, the religious Supreme Court and legislature of the Jewish people. It will be this court that will be able to formally recognize the Mashiach as the king of Israel.

When the Jewish people resided in Israel before the destruction of the Temple in Yerushalayim, they were governed by a supreme court called the Sanhedrin. Once the Jews were exiled this court ceased to exist, as it only had full authority when the Temple stood in Yerushalayim. This court is also crucial in the unfolding of the Messianic events because only it can formally recognize the Mashiach as the king of Israel.

Mission Six: He will restore the sacrificial system as well as the practices of the Shemittah, Sabbatical Year, and the Yovel, Jubilee Year.

All the laws connected to the Temple in Yerushalayim were suspended following its destruction. This included the sacrificial system that was a main part of the Temple's service. In addition, many of the agricultural laws had to be suspended as well due to the exile from the Land of Israel. The service in the Temple and agricultural laws will be reinstated with the coming of the Mashiach.

WHO IS THIS MASHIACH?

According to the Rambam,

> *If there arises a ruler from the family of David, immersed in Torah and its commandments like David his ancestor, following both the Written and Oral Torah, who leads Israel back to the Torah, strengthening the observance of its laws and fighting G-d's battles, then we may assume that he is the Mashiach. If he is further successful in rebuilding the Temple on its original site and gathering the dispersed of Israel, then his identity as the Mashiach is a certainty.*[40]

In the following chapters, we will delve more deeply into the six tasks of the Mashiach to discover how each one of them will play out with the Mashiach's revelation.

During the course of history many people have either claimed themselves to be Mashiach, or other people claimed about them that they were the Mashiach. Needless to say, none of them became the Mashiach, as the six accomplishments listed above are the **minimum** needed for our acceptance of anyone as the Mashiach. A brief look at the world today makes it clear that all previous people calling themselves the Mashiach were false as they did not achieve these minimal goals.

---

40   Rambam, *Mishneh Torah, Melachim* 11:4.

Chapter Three

THE ROLE OF THE JEWISH KING

AS WE ALREADY mentioned, the Mashiach will be the king of the Jewish people. What exactly is the role of the Jewish king? Why do the Jewish people need a king at all? Why isn't it sufficient to have courts of law and to follow G-d's commandments?

To explain the role of the Jewish king, we need to understand how the Torah describes the mission of a Jewish king. One of the 613 commandments in the Torah is to appoint a king over Israel. The Torah describes this mitzvah in the following way: "When you come into the Land that Hashem your G-d gives you and you take possession of it and dwell in it, and you say: 'I would set a king over me like all the other nations around me.'"[41]

In his commentary on the Bible, Chief Rabbi of the British Empire, Rabbi Dr. J.H. Hertz, describes the power of the Jewish king in the following way:

> *Among all other Oriental peoples, the word "king" connotes an irresponsible despot, vested with unchallenged authority. All law is the expression of his will. And while it binds every other member of the community, the monarch is free to disregard or to supersede it. He owes nothing to his subjects, and is not*

---

41   *Devarim* 17:14.

*answerable to anyone for his actions. In that world, the idea of
a "limited monarchy" was a contradiction in terms.*

*It was otherwise in Israel. It is G-d Who is the real King, and the
sole supreme authority. The monarch is the agent of the Divine
King, entrusted with the mission for which he is responsible to
G-d who chose him.*[42]

The king is therefore answerable not only to the people he leads but
to G-d who appointed him.

The Rambam writes about this mitzvah: "The Jews were charged with
three commandments upon entering the Land: to appoint a king, to cut
off the seed of the nation Amalek, and to build the Beis Hamikdash, the
Temple in Yerushalayim."[43]

The commandment makes it quite clear that it is not the purpose
of a king to serve as a charismatic warrior uniting the nation behind
him, meting out judgment to the enemies of the Jewish people. Nor
is it the king's job to even conquer and secure the Land of Israel for
the people. We know this because it was only *after* they had conquered
and secured the land and inhabited most of it that they had to appoint
a king in the first place.

G-d Himself had promised the Jewish people that they would enter
the Land of Israel and that they would be successful in their new homeland.[44] The Torah itself guaranteed that security, prosperity, and happiness would be found in the Land as a natural consequence of observing
the commandments, not for allegiance to a head of state or any mortal
leader, no matter how great and even righteous he would be.

Josephus Flavius, the Jewish historian who wrote and recorded for the
Romans, described the unique concept of a Jewish government like this:

*Some nations place the sovereignty of their land in the hands of
a single ruler (monarchy), some in the hands of a small number*

---

42   Rabbi Dr. J.H. Hertz, commentary on the Bible, pg. 927.
43   Rambam, *Sefer HaMitzvos, Mitzvos Asei* 20.
44   *Devarim* 28:1–14.

of rulers (oligarchy), and some in the hands of the people (democracy). Moshe Rabbeinu taught us to place our faith in none of these forms of government. He taught us to obey the rule of G-d, for to G-d alone did he attribute kingship and power. He commanded the people to always raise their eyes to G-d for He is the source of all good for mankind in general and for each person in particular, and in Him will people find help when they pray to Him in their time of suffering.[45]

People mistakenly understand Josephus's description of Jewish government as a form of theocracy, but in truth it isn't. The Jewish people were never meant to be led politically by a ruling class of priests but by G-d. Whether a king, a judge (as in the era before the kings), or no one leader rules over the Jewish people, the true King is the G-d of Israel. Whichever human has his hands on the reins of government is to be G-d's vehicle in this world.

WHAT IS THE CENTRAL ROLE OF A JEWISH KING?

The essential function of the king is to safeguard the Torah and to see to it that the people study it and obey its commandments. He did this by example. The king had tremendous power and privilege but was bound by the same Torah as the rest of the Jewish people. He was expected to live a scrupulous life with complete adherence to the Torah and the mitzvos. At the same time, certain unique powers were given to the king to assist him in carrying out his mission as leader of the Jewish people.

Based on the work of the Rambam,[46] these laws can be divided into two categories:

1) Sovereign Power

As the sovereign of the nation, the king is entitled to respect and reverence exceeding anyone else in the nation. People were expected to

---

45   Josephus, *Contra Appion.*
46   Rambam, *Mishneh Torah, Melachim* 3.

step aside to make way for him and even property may be destroyed for his convenience. As such, the king may not forfeit any of his prerogatives, as doing so would demean the nation he leads.

2) Special Powers

The king has extra-legal powers to confiscate, punish, and even to condemn to execution those he felt were treasonous in their actions. A Jewish court of law was not permitted to execute a murderer without a set of extraordinary strict rules of evidence and testimony. A king, however, may have a murderer killed as long as sufficient proof exists, even if circumstantial. Whoever is disrespectful or defiant of the king is liable to the death penalty upon his command.

All this, says the Rambam, was to ensure that he has the power to cast fear into the hearts and destroy the power of evildoers.[47]

In a perfect world, the Jewish king ascends his throne in a time of tranquility. The Jewish people are secure in their land and are observing the commandments exactly as G-d had commanded in the Torah. The king plays a unique role. He is first a citizen of the nation and is the living embodiment of the Torah and its teachings. At the same time, the king had tremendous power. Actually, part of the qualifications to become king of Israel is his duty to the nation to hold great wealth, to exhibit pomp, and to acquire what he needs to achieve his goals.

At the same time, he must shun any excess and he must be a perfect example of self-control and restraint in all his endeavors. All of the king's possessions were there to assist him in ruling his people with selfless service and to represent G-d on high in this world. The way he conducted his dealings with foreign nations, his business, family life, and daily interactions were expected to be according to Torah law and of the highest standards of honesty and morality. So the king's role was to be the prime living example of greatness that a person could see in this world. The king didn't just represent himself; he represented the Torah, his leadership reflected the will of the people, and his monarchy was a tribute to G-d Himself.

---

47   Ibid.

This idea explains why among all the mitzvos in the Torah, the king had a unique mitzvah to follow that no one else in the kingdom did, specifically to write two Torah scrolls:

- One of them he was commanded to keep in his palace.
- The other he carried around with himself at all times.

Just like a president of the United States of America carrying a copy of the US Constitution wherever he went, the carrying of a Torah symbolized where the king received his power from, i.e., G-d, and whom he is responsible for, i.e., the Jewish people.

What's crucial to understand in this description of the king's role is that the king was bestowed as a gift to the Jewish people by G-d. If they were worthy, they were given a great king befitting of their desire for greatness. However, if they were not, they were ruled by ruthless kings who had their own agendas and reasons for leadership. David HaMelech, an unknown shepherd who was unappreciated by his own family, became the true vision of what a Jewish king could achieve for G-d and the Jewish people and the important role a king can play in Jewish history.

Had the people been worthy, David would have been the final Mashiach and he would have built the one and only Temple of G-d in Yerushalayim. Sadly, the people did not merit this. True and final salvation would only come through his heirs and his eventual descendant, who would be known by the title Mashiach ben David, Mashiach son of David.[48]

To fully understand the Mashiach, we must become familiar with his direct ancestor by whose name he is called, David HaMelech.

---

48 Rabbi Samson Raphael Hirsch, *Devarim* 17:14.

Chapter Four

DAVID THE KING AND DAVID THE MAN

THE TALMUD TELLS us that *David Melech Yisrael Chai VeKayam* — David, king of Israel, lives and endures.[49] Even though he died nearly three thousand years ago, the legacy of David HaMelech lives on. The crowning accomplishment that drove David HaMelech was the building of the Temple in Yerushalayim. This was a building he knew he would never see. The *Mechilta* points out that the Book of *Tehillim* refers to the Temple as "The Temple by David."[50]

Asks the *Mechilta*, "But was David the one who built it? It was Shlomo HaMelech his son who built it! But because David devoted himself to building it, it was named after him."[51]

Since David was a man of war, he could not build the Temple, which was a House of Peace. He was permitted and able to lay the foundations.[52] However, his son Shlomo HaMelech, who never had to fight the wars of G-d, would be the one designated to build the holy Temple in Yerushalayim.

Two Davids emerge from Scriptures:

- David the king — a warrior and political unifier

---

49   *Rosh Hashanah* 25a.
50   *Tehillim* 30:1.
51   *Mechilta, Beshalach.*
52   *Shir HaShirim Rabbah* 1:6.

- David the flesh-and-blood human being — with struggles and his share of opponents, suffering, and domestic heartache

Either way, David HaMelech was a pivotal prime mover in G-d's plan of Creation: the one who was chosen to forge Israel's destiny, be instrumental in erecting the Temple, and in preparing the world for the eventual Mashiach. By saying, "David HaMelech lives and endures," we are referring to this David. He is not simply a mortal human being who strode the stage of history millennia ago and now survives in history books. He is still alive. David transcends the era in which he was alive because his ideals still move his people and because the Messianic destiny springs from him.

In his book, *David King of Israel*, Dr. Henry Biberfeld beautifully describes David HaMelech at his essence in the following way:

In David's life, ideas and above all the idea of the omnipresence of G-d, acquired a singular actuality. The awareness of the Divine occupied his existence to such a degree that it completely overshadowed all other aspects of being. Where others perceived a world made and moved by concrete facts and forces, and where, if recognized at all, the forces of the spirit led a shadowy existence in the background of reality, David saw a different world. To him it was a world of the spirit, of the all-pervading and all-sustaining reality of the Divine, animating and ennobling the mechanism of the universe. The invisible reality was his true reality. The world of the idea was his world. All his thoughts and feelings his words and actions, his wishes and impulses, were directed by the influences of that unseen reality.

Painfully slow, in a development that extended over many centuries and lands, the idea of preparing the world as the Kingdom of G-d on earth was absorbed into the organism of the Jewish people. Releases occurred, stagnation set in, other ideas took hold, the allure of the material achievements beckoned.

But beneath all this, the idea once it had taken root never died. It had become close, human, attainable. The impetus it received by the appearance of its human prototype carried it on through the nation's decline and exile.

This idea, hope and inner certainty, aim and essence of individual and national being, is to the Jew materialized in the immortal king. Thus, as once an idea had become the very being of David, now the being of David became the idea of the Jewish people. As David was sent to prove and proclaim in word and deed the omnipresence of the Divine on earth, thus Israel was sent into the world as herald of the Kingdom of G-d. David's message was taken over by the Jewish nation. His wondrous deeds and inspired songs which expressed his inner essential person became the vital reality, the distinctive feature of the Jewish people.[53]

Let's examine how David rose from young shepherd to David, *Melech Yisrael.*

KINGSHIP TRANSFERS FROM SHAUL TO DAVID

Shaul was commanded to destroy all remnants of Amalek from the earth. It says in the Book of Shmuel that Shmuel HaNavi said to Shaul, "Hashem sent me to anoint you as king over His people, over Israel, so now hear the sound of Hashem's words. So said Hashem, Master of Legions: 'I have remembered what Amalek did to Israel — the ambush he placed on them on the way, as they went up from Egypt. Now go and strike down Amalek and destroy everything he has.'"[54] The Radak writes that Shaul was first reminded that he was king of Israel and then told to attack Amalek, as if to say that his role as king of Israel was to follow G-d's command and lead the fight against Amalek.[55]

---

53   Dr. Henry Biberfeld, *David King of Israel* (Spero Foundation, 1963), pp. 8–9.
54   *Shmuel I* 15:1–3.
55   Radak, ibid. v. 1.

The connection between Shaul's position of king and the command to wipe out the nation of Amalek explains why his failure to completely fulfill that mission by not destroying the entire nation of Amalek led to his losing the position of king and its passing to David and his tribe Yehudah forever. Although David HaMelech had made mistakes during his tenure as king, they were considered as personal mistakes with no bearing on his role as monarch. Shaul's mistake was related to his position as king of Israel, and thereby his failure to complete that mission directly affected his ability to remain as king.[56]

Shaul's failure to do G-d's bidding was not an act of rebellion but of misplaced mercy: "Shaul, as well as the people, took pity on Agag (King of Amalek), on the best of the sheep, the cattle, the fatted bulls, the fatted sheep, and on all that was good; and they were not willing to destroy them; but the inferior livestock they did destroy." This was due to his extreme humility, as Shmuel told him, "Though you may be small in your own eyes, you are the head of the tribes of Israel; and Hashem has anointed you to be king over Israel."[57] His humility led to the continuation of the nation of Amalek, as that one extra night of life allowed Agag to bring offspring to the world.

G-d told Shmuel HaNavi, "I have reconsidered My having made Shaul king, for he has turned away from Me and has not fulfilled My word!"[58] To be the king of Israel needs humility, but not following the word of G-d through His prophet because of shortsighted human compassion led to the downfall of Shaul as king of Israel.

Soon after this episode, G-d tells Shmuel to "fill your horn with oil and go forth — I shall send you to Yishai from Beis Lechem, for I have seen a king for Myself among his sons."[59] Yishai presented his seven sons to Shmuel, but Shmuel realized that none of them was the chosen one; "Hashem has not chosen these."[60] Yishai did have a youngest son

---

56   *Sefer Ha'Ikarim* 24:4.
57   *Shmuel I* 15:17.
58   Ibid. v. 11
59   Ibid. 16:1
60   Ibid. v. 10.

who was tending to the sheep, his name was David. Upon meeting him, Shmuel realized he had found the leader of Israel. Hashem told Shmuel to "'arise and anoint him, for this is he!' Shmuel took the horn of oil and anointed him from among his brothers, and the spirit of Hashem passed over David from that day on."[61]

DAVID HAMELECH AND YERUSHALAYIM

Upon becoming king of a united Israel, David made the conquest of Yerushalayim his first priority. According to the Radak, there was a tradition in Israel that Yerushalayim would never be conquered until all the Jewish people would be united under one king.[62] When David was king over only Yehudah, Chevron was the best location for his capital, being that Chevron was located in the heartland of Yehudah's territory. But now that he was king over all of Israel, he relocated his center of government to Yerushalayim.

David wanted so much to build the Temple in Yerushalayim, as it says, "The king said to Nasan HaNavi, 'See, now I am dwelling in a house of cedar, while the Ark of G-d dwells within curtains!'"[63] However, Hashem did not permit David to build it: "When your days are complete and you lie with your forefathers, I shall raise up after you your offspring who will issue from your loins, and I shall make firm the throne of his kingdom forever."[64] Although we are not told here in the Book of Shmuel why David HaMelech was prevented from building the Temple, elsewhere, David charges his son Shlomo with the responsibility of building the Temple.[65] He explains to Shlomo that he had been forbidden to build the Temple because he was a man of war who had shed much blood, and the Temple was a place of peace, and so his son Shlomo was given the permission to build it.

Even so, David and not Shlomo was shown the Temple's location. David also purchased the land, and as the last eight chapters of *Divrei*

---

61   Ibid. v. 12.

62   *Shmuel II* 5:6.

63   Ibid. 7:1.

64   Ibid. v. 12.

65   *Divrei HaYamim II* 22:7-8.

HaYamim recount, David plunged into the task of preparing the necessary resources for Shlomo HaMelech's future construction. For this reason the Temple is called "David's House."[66]

DAVID AND HIS TEMPLE

Although David HaMelech was not permitted to build the Temple, he is inextricably linked to it. The Temple was built on Har HaMoriah in Yerushalayim, which David had set up to be the eternal capital of the Jewish people. This is why the Rambam states that from the time the Temple was built in Yerushalayim, it is forbidden to build a Tabernacle or altar anywhere else.[67] Only Har HaMoriah in Yerushalayim is the proper site of the Temple.

It was also only in David's merit that the Holy Ark, which contained the Ten Commandments, was permitted to enter the Temple at all. The Talmud tells us that when Shlomo HaMelech built the Temple, he sought to bring the Ark into the Holy of Holies, but the gates miraculously sealed shut and could not be opened! When Shlomo HaMelech saw this, he recited twenty-four songs of prayer, but the gates still remained shut. After many attempts of various prayers, Shlomo HaMelech said, "Hashem, G-d! Don't turn away the face of Your anointed one! Remember the pieties of David your servant,"[68] and he was immediately answered and the gates opened.[69] This was a public vindication of David's righteousness and proof that Shlomo HaMelech was his successor — not only on the throne, but as the builder of the Temple.

THE PROMISE TO DAVID OF ETERNAL KINGSHIP

G-d promised David that his monarchy would last in perpetuity. When the prophet relates what G-d said about David's kingship, he

---

66　*Tehillim* 30:1.
67　Rambam, *Mishneh Torah*, Laws of the Temple 1:3.
68　*Divrei HaYamim II* 6:42.
69　*Shabbos* 30a.

writes, "If I were to break My covenant with day and night, that day or night would no longer come in their appointed time, then also would My covenant with David break, that he should have a son reigning upon his throne."[70] So the Messianic era is the focus of world history and is the purpose and justification of Creation. David is deeply connected and identified as the progenitor of the kingly line that would end with the Mashiach himself. From the moment David was promised the kingship, he was transformed from an individual in one time and place into a figure of eternity.

David was so humbled by this promise that he sat down before G-d (which Rashi tells us means he sat before the Ark) and said, "Who am I, O Hashem G-d, and who is my house that You have brought me to this point?"[71] The Talmud tells us he is talking about his personal kingship being granted to him and in perpetuity to his family. As David says in the next verse, "So that You spoke concerning the house of Your servant into the distant future."[72] This promise was not limited to David himself, but passed to his descendants. The Mashiach and his kingship are therefore so connected to David HaMelech that he is referred to as Mashiach son of David. That is the impact David had not only on his time but all of Jewish history.

---

70   *Yirmiyah* 33:20–1.
71   *Divrei HaYamim I* 17:16.
72   Ibid. v. 17.

Chapter Five

THE FOUR EXILES

ONE OF THE key features of Jewish history is the many exiles the nation of Israel has been forced to endure. We have experienced four main exiles that included many other smaller ones. This means that on four occasions we were either expelled from Israel by a conquering nation or remained in Israel while the Land of Israel was overrun and controlled by a conquering nation. Each time we were put into exile, the Jewish people suffered very greatly, having to leave their homes and families and suffering much death and destruction wrought upon their bodies. On two of those occasions, exile went hand-in-hand with the destruction of the First and Second Temples in Yerushalayim.

If exile has been such a central feature of the Jewish experience, there must be a deeper reason for it. What is the purpose of exile?

The most well-known reason for exile is sin, as we say in our holiday *Mussaf* prayers: "Because of our sins You exiled us from our land." The idea is that living safely in Israel is a privilege and not a right. If we sin, we lose our merit to reside peacefully in the Land.

The Talmud gives a second reason for exile: "Rabbi Yosi said, the Son of David (i.e., Mashiach) will not come before all the souls in the *guf* have been emptied out."[73] The word *guf* literally means "body," but it is also a reference to the storehouse where all the souls reside before they

---

73   *Niddah* 13b.

enter this world. According to Rabbi Yosi, then, the Redemption will not come until no unborn souls remain in heaven.

According to the Ramban, this is because every soul needs a chance to be rewarded for its good deeds.[74] Reward can only be given to those souls that have experienced and exercised their free will. This world is the only place where free will is given, and once the Mashiach comes, free will can no longer exist. So according to the Ramban, Mashiach can only come once every soul has had a chance to fight and win over its free will.

ATTRACTING CONVERTS

A third reason why the Jewish people have been put into exile is not so much what it does for us but what it does for those nations we are connected to in exile. The Talmud makes the following remarkable statement, "Rabbi Elazar said, the Holy One, Blessed Be He, exiled Israel among the nations in order that proselytes might join them."[75] The Talmud is thus telling us that the Jewish people would have to leave the comfort and safety of Israel in order to attract potential converts to the Jewish faith who are residing among the other nations.

Think about it: how would a non-Jew in Egypt, Russia, France, the United States, or anywhere else in the world know about the Jewish faith without seeing a Jew living near them? The Maharsha concurs with this reason for the exile of the Jewish people from Israel, stating that sin cannot be the sole reason for exile, because many other forms of punishment were available to "take care of" sin. Rather, the purpose of exile is to attract converts and to publicize our faith in G-d to other nations.[76]

Perhaps, then, exile plays a dual purpose. We find ourselves in exile because of our mistakes, but once we are there, we are expected to be a "light unto the nations" and allow those souls dispersed around the

---

74   *Devarim* 30:6.

75   *Pesachim* 87b.

76   Maharsha, *Chiddushei Aggados, Pesachim* 87b.

world to learn about G-d and potentially become part of the Jewish nation itself.

Indeed, exile is so fundamental to the progress of the world that it appears in the Torah: we see in the Torah itself that exile was to become part of Jewish history by seeing what happened to the Patriarchs themselves. Of all the Patriarchs, one stood out from the others in helping us understand exile. That patriarch was Yaakov.

YAAKOV THE EXILED PATRIARCH

Of all the patriarchs, Yaakov represented the Jewish people in exile. Unlike his father Yitzchak, Yaakov was the one who had to spend much of his life outside the Land of Israel, dealing with all the trials and tribulations that comes with being a foreigner on foreign land. Let's examine one of the main exiles that Yaakov went through when fleeing from his brother Eisav when traveling to live with his uncle Laban, and by doing so we will discover the root of all the future exiles of the Jewish people.

YAAKOV'S LADDER AND THE FOUR ANGELS

Before he died, Yitzchak wanted to bless his son Eisav. Yaakov and his mother Rivka realized that Eisav was not worthy of these blessings after the disastrous life decisions he had made, including selling Yaakov his birthright for a pot of beans. Yaakov took advantage of his father Yitzchak's old age, and tricked him into giving him Eisav's blessing. This was Rivka's idea, and she was right to suggest it. When Eisav realized what had happened, he was furious and threatened to kill his brother Yaakov. Yaakov was forced to flee for his life and live with his uncle Laban outside of Israel.

On the way there, he stopped to spend the night on Har HaMoriah. This was the very same mountain his grandfather Avraham had brought his father Yitzchak as a potential sacrifice many years before. It was holy ground. Upon awakening, he referred to this special place as *Shaar HaShamayim*, the Gateway to Heaven. This mountain was one day to be chosen by David HaMelech as the home of the Holy Temple in Yerushalayim.

When Yaakov slept, he dreamt of a ladder. The ladder was rooted firmly on the ground and its top reached up into the heavens. In the dream Yaakov saw angels ascending and descending the ladder. These angels, says the Midrash, were the guardian angels of the four kingdoms — Bavel, Madai, Yavan, and Romi (Babylon, Media, Greece, and Rome) — that were to ascend and dominate over Yaakov's descendants, i.e., the Jewish people, at various points in history.[77] The *Baal HaTurim* gives a hint to this by showing how the numerical value of the words used by the Torah — *olim v'yordim*, ascending and descending — are the same as the numerical value for the Hebrew words Bavel, Madai, Yavan, and Romi; both are 428.[78]

Yaakov saw each angel climb the number of rungs corresponding to the years of its dominion, and then descend, signaling the end of its reign:

- Babylon's angel climbed seventy rungs and then went down.
- Media's angel climbed fifty-two rungs and then descended.
- The Greek angel climbed one hundred and thirty rungs and then descended.
- However, the final angel, representing the fourth kingdom Edom, which descended from Eisav, kept climbing indefinitely, symbolizing our current exile, which has lasted for two thousand plus years, seemingly never ending.

This frightened Yaakov until G-d reassured him that he would receive Divine protection and that even that last kingdom would eventually fall, and the Jews would return to Israel at the End of Days.

Yaakov resumed his journey. He ended up marrying his cousins, Rachel and Leah, as well as being swindled many times over in business by their father, his unscrupulous uncle Laban.

Yaakov's journey out of Israel is a microcosm of his descendants' eventual exile from the Land of Israel. However, if Yaakov represents the exile, he also represents the return. It is for this reason that Yaakov

---

77   *Vayikra Rabbah* 29:2.
78   *Bereishis* 28:13.

was one of the only people privy to know the end date of the exile and when the Mashiach's arrival would be.

On his deathbed, Yaakov was about to reveal this information to his children but was prevented from doing so by G-d. The exact time of the end has remained a mystery ever since then.

YAAKOV'S DESCENT TO EGYPT AND ITS PARALLEL TO THE REDEMPTION

Based on the principle of *maaseh avos siman lebanim*, the actions of the forefathers serve as a model for future generations, the Ramban writes that Yaakov's descent into Egypt and eventual burial in Israel serve as a model for our current exile and future redemption.[79] He identifies numerous parallels between Yaakov's exile to Egypt and our current exile at the hands of Edom. Here are his words:

> *I have already mentioned that Yaakov's descent to Egypt parallels our current exile in the hands of Rome, Edom.*
>
> 1. *Yaakov's sons themselves caused their descent to Egypt through their sale of their brother Yosef.*
> 2. *Yaakov descended there because of famine.*
> 3. *He thought only to be saved from the starvation with his son Yosef in the house of one who loved him, for Pharaoh loved Yosef, and Yosef was like his son.*
> 4. *Yaakov's children intended to return to their homeland as soon as the famine ended, as it says, "We have come to sojourn in the land since there is no grazing for your servants' flocks for the famine is intense in the Land of Canaan." But they did not go back; the exile became protracted.*
> 5. *Yaakov died there and only his bones went up.*
> 6. *The elders of Pharaoh brought him back.*
> 7. *And made for him a "grievous mourning."*

---

79   *Bereishis* 47:28.

Likewise, we are with Rome and Edom:

1. *Our brothers the Chashmona'im caused our coming under their control, for they made a pact with the Romans.[80]*

2. *And Agrippa II, the last king of the Second Temple period, fled to them for assistance.[81] [Parallel to 3 above]*

3. *And, because of the famine, the people of Yerushalayim were captured by the Romans. [Parallel to 2 above]*

4. *And the exile has become extremely protracted for us. We don't know its end, though we did in other exiles.*

5. *We are like dead men, exclaiming, "Our bones are dried out...we are doomed."[82]*

6. *But in the end, "They will bring us up from among all the nations, a tribute to G-d."[83]*

7. *And they will have a "grievous mourning" upon seeing our glory. We will see G-d's vengeance, may He preserve us and we will live before Him.*

The comparison is quite astonishing. Just as the Egyptians participate in the burial of Yaakov, showing great honor, so too there will be a universal recognition of G-d and His people that will take place

---

80 Yehudah Maccabee sought an alliance with the Roman Republic to remove the Greeks. Josephus reports: "In the year 161 BCE he sent Eupolemus the son of Yochanan and Jason the son of Elazar to make a league of amity and confederacy with the Romans." (*Jewish War*, translation adapted from that of William Whiston.) Later, Jonathan sought alliances with foreign peoples. He renewed the treaty with the Roman Republic. Hyraces II and Aristobulus II, Simon's great-grandsons, became pawns in a proxy war between Julius Caesar and Pompey the Great. See *Yosipon*, chaps. 23, 45.

81 The later Herodian rulers Agrippa I and Agrippa II both had Hasmonean blood, as Agrippa I's father was Aristobulus IV, son of Herod by Mariamne I, but they were not direct male descendants of the Chashmona'im. During the first Jewish-Roman war of 66–73, Agrippa sent soldiers to support Vespasian, showing that although Jewish in religion, he was devoted to the Romans. The Ramban means that just as Yosef depended on the friendship of Pharaoh, so too Agrippa relied on his friendship of Rome. *Yosipon*, chap. 64.

82 *Yechezkel* 37:11.

83 *Yeshayah* 66:20.

at the time of the Redemption when the non-Jews will participate in and contribute to the Final Redemption. The Ramban compares the Jewish people before the coming of the Mashiach to a corpse, just like Yaakov died in the exile of Egypt. But like the dry bones of Yechezkel's vision, so too will the Jewish people be reinvigorated at the time of the Redemption.

DANIEL AND HIS VISION OF THE FOUR BEASTS

Many years later, each one of these four exiles was seen by the prophet Daniel. Note that he was one of the only people who knew when the final Messianic Redemption would occur and was himself part of the first exile.

Each of the four kingdoms came to him in a vision in the form of terrifying creatures, each one scarier and more frightening than the one before it. These creatures can't be called animals, because the form by which they were revealed to Daniel was far from that of a regular animal.

Belshazzar, the grandson of Nebuchadnezzar, was king of Babylon when Daniel received these prophecies, and they can be found in the Book of Daniel, chapter 7.

The vision began with four mighty winds, each coming from one of the four directions of the world, and each one stirring up the Great Sea, the Mediterranean. In order to understand the Messianic Redemption at the End of Days, it's important to examine these four beasts carefully, as every detail of these creatures reveals something unique about the exile:

Beast One represented the exile of Babylon and appeared to Daniel like a lion with eagle's wings. The lion was used as a metaphor because lions have tremendous power. The wings of the eagle represent the great speed and energy by which the Babylonians were able to complete their conquests. The Babylonians destroyed the First Temple built by Shlomo HaMelech after it stood in Yerushalayim for four hundred and ten years.

The prophet then tells us that eventually "its wings were plucked and it was removed from the earth." This plucking represents the destruction of the Babylonians by the Persians and Medes, who were not powerful enough to subdue the Babylonians under Nebuchadnezzar, but were able to destroy them under the reign of Belshazzar, which is when Daniel lived.

Beast Two represented the Persian exile and appeared to Daniel like a bear. This came out of the ocean second. The Persians did not possess great power like the Babylonians, nor their agility, but were likened to a bear, which is not noted for its great speed but is still a powerful and corpulent animal. The Persians were not regal like their predecessors the Babylonians and therefore were not compared to the lion.

In its mouth were three ribs. Each rib represented a different king — Cyrus, Achashverosh, and Darius. The second king, Achashverosh, was the leader who ruled over 127 provinces from India to Ethiopia. The Purim story (as told in *Megillas Esther*) relates the story of Mordechai and Esther and their dealings with Achashverosh, which culminated with the Jewish people's miraculous redemption from the evil machinations of the Amalakite Haman. Soon after, the Jewish people were permitted by Darius to return to Israel and rebuild the Second Temple.

Beast Three represented the Greek exile and appeared as a leopard with four heads, as well as four wings growing out of its back. The leopard represented the distinguished and brilliant reign of Alexander the Great, who conquered most of Asia in one continuous swoop like a ferocious leopard. The speed by which Alexander the Great conquered so much territory in such a short time (twelve years) and during such a short lifespan (he died by the age of thirty-two) was represented by the four wings on his back, which are like the four directions in which Alexander moved.

After his death, Alexander was succeeded by four generals who divided his empire. These generals were: Ptolemy who took Egypt; Seleucas who took Assyria and Babylon, Antigonas who took Persia and Asia Minor, and Phillip (Alexander's brother) who took Macedonia. These were the four heads that were on Daniel's leopard.

The Syrian-Greeks overran Israel and defiled the Temple, bringing a pig into the Holy of Holies. As we know from the famous Chanukah story, the Maccabees fought back and recaptured the Second Temple from their hands, rededicating the Temple by lighting the Menorah, which only had enough light for one day but miraculously lasted for eight days.

Beast Four (the last) was the Roman exile. Daniel describes the Roman Empire as a beast which is "excessively terrifying, awesome and strong; with immense iron teeth, and ten horns." The seeming redundancy of the words "terrifying" and "awesome" corresponds to the double nature of the fourth kingdom, i.e., the rise of both Christianity and Islam.

In the vision, the beast "ate and crumbled" using the large iron teeth, symbolizing the rulers of Rome and the emperors who crushed and digested many other nations into themselves. The beast also "trampled the rest with its feet"; this represented the other nations that were not destroyed by the Roman Empire but instead brutally beaten into submission.

What about the ten horns? Each one of these horns represented a different Roman emperor. These emperors were: Julius Caesar,[84] Augustus, Tiberias, Caligula, Claudius, Nero, Galba, Otho, Vitellius, and Vespasian (Aspasyanus). During his father Vespasian's reign, Titus destroyed the Second Temple in Yerushalayim.

Daniel continues his vision by examining these ten horns and then seeing another small horn coming up, which uprooted three of the previous horns. Who the small horn refers to is a matter of great debate:

- Some say that it is a reference to Titus who destroyed the Temple, even though he was small in stature since he was not an emperor.
- Others however understand this to be the papacy. Although it would be many years until the Roman Church would have the power to make its presence felt, eventually the power of the

---

84   Julius Caesar was not an emperor, but his power equaled that of an emperor since he was made a dictator for life.

Church would rise up until the popes of the Middle Ages were able to challenge even the most powerful rulers.

- Others interpret that this part of the prophecy has not yet come true and is a reference to a nation that will one day convert to Islam and will come up against the Christian world.

This leads us to what some describe as the fifth and final exile, which according to some will be short but more painful than the previous exiles.[85]

---

85   **The Messianic Code:** The Midrash (*Pirkei D'Rebbi Eliezer* 48) states that the identity of the final Mashiach was known to the Patriarchs and was handed down from generation to generation, but was forbidden to be revealed to those who weren't privy to that information. It was tied to the five letters of the *aleph-beis* that have two forms, one as it appears in the beginning or middle of the word, the other as it appears at the end of the word. These five letters are *chaf, mem, nun, pey,* and *tzadi*. Each of these five letters are actually pairs. These five are also related to a different redemption. Let's see how.
The letter *chaf* appears twice in conjunction with G-d's command to Avraham to leave the land of his birth and go to Canaan; *lech lecha.*
The letter *mem* appears twice in Avimelech's words to Yitzchak, when he told him to leave Gerar, "For you have become much mightier *mimenu,* than us."
The letter *nun* appears twice in Yaakov's prayer that he be saved from Eisav, *hatzileini na.*
The letter *pey* was used twice regarding the redemption from Egypt, *pakod pakadeti.*
The final letter, *tzadi,* is a reference to the future redemption of the Jewish people at the End of Days. As Zechariah the Prophet states (6:12), "Behold there is a man, his name is Tzemach, and he will flourish (*yitzmach*)."
This code, says the *Baal HaTurim* (*Bereishis* 37:3), informs us that Yaakov did give Yosef knowledge regarding the end of the exile.

Chapter Six

THE FIFTH EXILE OF ADAM

WE SAW THE four exiles to which the Jewish people have been subjected. We also saw how the prophet compared each of these four exiles to a different animal. We shall now see how a fifth exile was predicted by the Sages, and how this exile will be the shortest but the most challenging of them all. This is the fifth exile of Adam.

> A fifth exile was predicted… the exile of Adam.

In order to understand the fifth exile, we need to travel back to the days of Avraham, his concubine Hagar, and their son Yishmael. The Torah tells us that G-d commanded Hagar to "call his name Yishmael…he will be a *pere adam*, a wild man. His hand will be on everything and the hand of everyone on him."[86] The Ramban says that these verses relate not so much to Yishmael but to his offspring wreaking havoc on everyone, and vice versa: "His descendants will wage war against all the nations."

The *Zohar* states, "And the sons of Yishmael (the Arabs) in that time (the pre-Messianic era) will fire the entire world to rise up against Yerushalayim. And all the nations will band together against the Jews to remove them from the Land and the world."[87] About this era it is written: "It will be a time of trouble for Yaakov (the Jews), but he shall be saved from it."[88]

---

86   *Bereishis* 16:11–12.
87   *Zohar*, book 1, 25a, 119a.
88   *Yirmiyah* 30:7.

The Torah's description of the descendants of Yishmael being a *pere adam* is very telling. The word *pere* means unbridled, wild, and unhinged, yet at the same time he is an *adam*, a man, unlike the four previous exiles that are compared to beasts. Yishmael is compared to a human, which is more dignified. However, since the Torah places the adjective *pere* before the proper noun *adam*, the emphasis is on the nature of his bad character, which happens to take the form of an *adam*. It is accepted by the Jewish commentators and others that the offspring of Yishmael is a reference to the Muslims, who see Yishmael as one of their most important spiritual ancestors.

Rabbi Chaim Vital, a leading disciple of the Arizal, Rabbi Yitzchak Luria, explains the fifth exile in the following way:

> *You already know that the exiles from Egypt until the Mashiach are four — Babylonia, Persia, Greece, and Rome. However, the Jewish people are destined further in the End of Days to be in the exile of Yishmael, the son of Avraham. Yishmael was circumcised, and is referred to as a pere adam, a wild ass of a man,[89] implying not a full man, because he was circumcised without periah (an integral part of the bris milah). But the other four exiles are compared to beasts as mentioned in the Book of Daniel.[90]*

David HaMelech prophesied with *ruach hakodesh*, a Divine spirit, when he said in Psalm 124:

1. A Song of Ascents of David.
2. If it had not been the Lord who was for us, let Israel now say;
3. If it had not been for the Lord who was for us, when a man (Adam) rose up over us;
4. Then they had swallowed us up alive, when their wrath was kindled against us.

---

89   *Bereishis* 16:12.
90   Rabbi Chaim Vital, *Etz Hadaas Tov, Tehillim* 124.

While the first four exiles can be seen in the words, "If it had not been the Lord who was for us," the next part, "man, Adam, rose up over us," is a reference to Yishmael, who is known as *adam*, the man. Yishmael is called "a man" because he is a son of Avraham and therefore has the merit of his forefather, as we find (Avraham praying for Yishmael to G-d): "Would that Yishmael live before You,"[91] and he also has the merit of the *milah* (circumcision). Due to this as well, he is called *adam*.

Therefore his exile is harder than the other four kingdoms, as our Sages have said: "Because for this he is called Yishmael, that in the future Yisrael will scream out, tremendous screams in the days of his exile, and *Yishma-El*, G-d will listen, and will answer them."

So according to Rabbi Chaim Vital, since Yishmael is a son of Avraham and his descendants circumcise their children, even though they are not commanded to, they have the merit of G-d listening to them and subjugating the Jewish people in Israel right until the Mashiach comes and takes back the Land of Israel from them.

He continues:

> *And afterwards Yishmael will rise and become king over the entire world, and over Israel. And this is what is meant by "when a man rose up over us."*[92]
>
> *And this is what Israel will say then: "If it had not been for the Lord who was for us, when a man (Adam) rose up over us," which is Yishmael, "then they had swallowed us up alive."*[93] *This means that during the fifth exile it will be different than all that passed over us. Because they will want to swallow us alive when their wrath will be kindled against us, they will desire to erase the name Israel from under the heavens, like something which is swallowed, whose existence is no longer noticeable at all and as if it never existed. They will not succeed, however, as G-d will hear our prayers and redeem us.*

---

91   *Bereishis* 17:18.
92   *Tehillim* ibid. v. 2.
93   Ibid. v. 3.

Although we will be subjugated in this fifth exile by the descendants of Yishmael (the Arabs), who have their own merits, this is only up until the Mashiach's arrival. Once the Mashiach reveals himself, the entire Land of Israel and the Temple Mount will revert to being the Jewish people's once again.

ROMAN AND ARAB EMPIRES SWEEP ACROSS THE WORLD

The Rambam had a very close relationship with the Jews of Yemen. To this day, Yemenite Jews follow the teachings of the Rambam and speak of him only with the greatest reverence. The reason for this is because the Rambam spent much time sending correspondence to the Jewish community of Yemen, guiding them, answering their questions and generally being their spiritual guide during some of the biggest challenges their community was facing from hostile elements within their country.

One example of the correspondence the Rambam wrote to the Jews of Yemen was the *Iggeres Teiman*, Letter to Yemen. The *Iggeres Teiman* was written in 1172 in Arabic as a response to an inquiry from Rabbi Yaakov ben Natanel Fayumi, who was the leader of the Jewish community in Yemen. In those days, a fanatical Shiite Muslim rebel had risen to power and was forcing the Jews to convert to Islam. Their choice was to either convert or face expulsion. To make matters worse, a charismatic Jewish man purporting to be the long-awaited Mashiach appeared on the scene. He began misleading the unlearned masses and gained quite a following. Many Jews of the day attempted to calculate the End of Days and the precise arrival time of the Mashiach through astrology.

The Rambam was sensitive to all these issues facing the community and began addressing each of their concerns in a letter that he sent to them. In it, he refuted the claims of the false Mashiach among them, listed the requisite requirement of anyone claiming to be the Mashiach, debunked any use of astrology to predict the Mashiach's arrival time, and finally offered great comfort to the Jews of Yemen to have faith in G-d during all their challenging times and to await the arrival of the true Mashiach.

The letter was read in public gatherings in every city and village, and they were able to successfully refute the supposed miracles of the false Mashiach. The Jews of Yemen resolved to remain faithful to their Judaism. To this day, Yemenite Jews have clung to the traditions of their forefathers despite ceaseless persecution, harassment, and oppression.

In the *Iggeres Teiman*, the Rambam says the following about the Arabs (as the descendants of Yishmael) at the End of Days:[94]

> *We know from the prophecies of Daniel and Yeshayah, and from the words of our Sages, that the Mashiach will come after the Roman and Arab empires have swept across the world. Only after Daniel spoke of the Arab empire and the rise of Mohammad did he speak of the coming of the Mashiach, which will take place afterward. Yeshayah also declared in his vision that the arrival of the Mashiach will be linked to the appearance of Mohammad when he says, "He will see mounted men, horsemen in pairs, riders on donkeys, riders on camels, and he will listen closely and attentively."[95]*

The rider on the donkey, explains the Rambam, is the Mashiach, as the prophet Zechariah described him, "Humble and riding on a donkey."[96] The Mashiach will come after the rise of the man riding the camel, that is, says the Rambam, the Arab empire.

MUSLIMS ARE ALSO TRUE MONOTHEISTS

Throughout history, it is only the descendants of Yishmael who, like the Jewish people, have practiced true monotheism. This explains the name Yishmael, which contains within in the Name of G-d, *El*. The Torah also refers to the leaders of Yishmael in the Torah as *nesi'im*, princes. However, everything they do in the worship of the One true G-d is extreme, unbridled. Their practice of modesty, while noble in theory,

---

94   Rambam, *Iggeres Teiman*, pgs. 49–50.
95   *Yeshayah* 21:7.
96   *Zechariah* 9:9.

ends up being oppressive. While Judaism speaks of self-sacrifice for a higher cause, this is rarely to be taken literally and refers to giving up our creature comforts and some of our income to take care of others.

Many of the descendants of Yishmael (Arabs) take this idea of self-sacrifice into the extreme and are willing to sacrifice their own physical lives for their beliefs, even though they are not commanded to by G-d, sometimes by killing in the name of G-d in the most appalling and non-G-dly ways known to man. This is not the path G-d wants, as we shall see.

Let us illustrate this from a very famous story in the Torah — that the last thing G-d actually wants is for people to commit suicide and to kill others in the name of G-d. The great person we are going to learn this lesson from is someone very respected by the three main religious faiths, i.e., Avraham Avinu.

> The last thing G-d actually wants is for people to commit suicide and to kill others in the name of G-d.

AVRAHAM TAKES YITZCHAK TO HAR HAMORIAH

One of the most powerful moments in the Torah is the episode of Avraham taking his one and only son from Sarah, Yitzchak, to Har HaMoriah. The Torah describes the story in the following way:[97]

> *And it came to pass after these things, that G-d tested Avraham, and He said to him, "Avraham," and he said, "Here I am." And He said, "Please take your son, your only one, whom you love, Yitzchak, and go away to the Land of Moriah and bring him up there for a burnt offering on one of the mountains, of which I will tell you."*
>
> *And Avraham arose early in the morning, and he saddled his donkey, and he took his two young men with him and Yitzchak his son; and he split wood for a burnt offering, and he arose and went to the place of which G-d had told him. On*

---

97   *Bereishis*, chap. 22.

the third day, Avraham lifted up his eyes and saw the place from afar. And Avraham said to his young men, "Stay here with the donkey, and I and the lad will go yonder, and we will prostrate ourselves and return to you." And Avraham took the wood for the burnt offering, and he placed it upon his son Yitzchak, and he took into his hand the fire and the knife, and they both went together.

And Yitzchak spoke to Avraham his father, and he said, "My father!" And he said, "Here I am, my son." And he said, "Here is the fire and the wood, but where is the lamb for the burnt offering?"

And Avraham said, "G-d will provide for Himself the lamb for the burnt offering, my son." And they both went together. And they came to the place of which G-d had spoken to him, and Avraham built the altar there and arranged the wood, and he bound Yitzchak his son and placed him on the altar upon the wood. And Avraham stretched forth his hand and took the knife, to slaughter his son. And an angel of G-d called to him from heaven and said, "Avraham! Avraham!" And he said, "Here I am."

And he said, "Do not stretch forth your hand to the lad, nor do the slightest thing to him, for now I know that you are a G-d-fearing man, and you did not withhold your son, your only one, from Me."

And Avraham lifted up his eyes, and he saw, and lo! there was a ram, it was caught in a tree by its horns. And Avraham went and took the ram and offered it up as a burnt offering instead of his son.

And Avraham named that place, "The Lord will see," as it is said to this day: On the mountain, the Lord will be seen.

And an angel of the Lord called to Avraham a second time from heaven. And he said, "By Myself have I sworn, says the Lord, that because you have done this thing and you did not withhold your son, your only one, that I will surely bless you, and I will greatly multiply your seed as the stars of the heavens and as the sand that is on the seashore, and your descendants will inherit the cities of their enemies. And through your children shall be blessed all the nations of the world, because you hearkened to My voice."

This story needs some understanding. Did G-d want Avraham to kill his son Yitzchak or not? If He did, did G-d just change His mind? According to the story, Avraham was more than ready to fulfill this command. If, however, G-d had no intention of having Avraham kill Yitzchak, why did He send him in the first place?

The many answers to these questions deserve a book in themselves. For now, let us understand that Avraham was being tested. This event was as real as could be for him and his son Yitzchak. They were not aware that G-d was going to "change His mind" and stop the entire process. They were willing and ready to go ahead with this devastating plan, painful though it was to Avraham knowing that he was about to lose his one and only son from Sarah and not see an entire set of descendants from her as he had hoped and prayed for.

This episode comes for two reasons, a test and a lesson. It was a test for Avraham and a lesson for us:

- The test, which Avraham passed with flying colors, was whether he was willing to permit his son Yitzchak to become a sacrifice.
- However, the lesson for us is wholly different; we are being told the exact opposite, i.e., don't kill your children for G-d!

Let me explain. In the days of Avraham Avinu, child sacrifice was part and parcel of idol worship. In order to appease the gods, priests of various idols such as *Molech* many times required that a person bring a sacrifice to the god in the form of their greatest treasure. They would throw their child into the fire and let the fire consume their child. These sacrifices were performed with musical instruments and loud chanting in order to drown out the horrific cries of the young child being burned alive.

What Avraham spent much of his life doing was telling people not to kill their children for G-d. The true G-d doesn't want us to die for His sake; He wants us to live for His sake. How would G-d demonstrate this idea? By asking the greatest and most famous spiritual leader of the day, i.e., Avraham, to climb a mountain with his son Yitzchak, for whom he and his wife Sarah had waited for so many years, and command him to **not** kill his son. This lesson was well known in the days of Avraham and was incorporated by G-d into the Torah to teach us and all peoples that G-d does not seek our death but our life.

This lesson is as important today as it was then: live for G-d. Living for G-d as opposed to dying for G-d is a much more challenging proposition. Anyone can fly a plane into a building or strap a bomb onto their back and kill themselves and many other innocent men, women, and children. Is this what G-d wants? Certainly not. Avraham demonstrated (rather than just taught) the importance of life. The greatest gift we have is life, and shortening it will not in any way bring the anticipated Mashiach. We hear of frequent suicide attacks being perpetrated by religious fanatics against innocent victims. Avraham demonstrated to us very clearly that trying to bring the end closer by killing others and sacrificing ourselves and our children is not what G-d wants.

Chapter Seven

WHAT'S IN A NAME? THE FOUR POSSIBLE NAMES OF THE MASHIACH

ALTHOUGH WE ARE not informed of who the Mashiach is until his arrival, the Talmud reveals to us what his name will be.[98] The Talmud goes as far as to tell us that "the name of the Mashiach was created before the world was created, as it is written about him: 'May his name endure forever; his name existed before the sun.'[99] The name of the Mashiach predated the creation of the sun and the rest of the world."[100]

Before we look at the personal names of the Mashiach, it is worth noting that a Hebrew name is not merely a means of identification; it's much more than that. A person's name can reveal much about whom they are and their mission in life. Let us understand this more deeply.

The Hebrew word for a soul is *neshamah*. The middle two letters of *neshamah* are *shem*, which means "name." A person's name does more than act as a way for people to identify themselves. Names contain the structure of the soul's mission in this world. Interestingly, we are told in the Kabbalistic writings that when parents name their child, they are given a certain amount of *Ruach HaKodesh*, Divine spirit, in order to give their child the correct name, which will match the child's

---

98   *Sanhedrin* 98b.
99   *Tehillim* 72:17.
100   *Nedarim* 39b.

personality and give him the formula he needs for spiritual success. Very much like the bar code on an item in the supermarket, which when passed over the red light at the checkout reveals much information about the item, such as its value, the facility it was made in, the expiration date and more, so too your Hebrew name contains within it crucial information about your personality, life purpose, and more. A person's physical existence is a tangible form of the essence his name expresses.

> Your Hebrew name contains crucial information about your personality, life purpose, and more.

YOUR NAME IS YOUR MISSION

The Midrash tells us that man is called by three different names: "The first is the one given him by his father and mother; the second is the one by which others call him. The third is the one by which he is inscribed in the Book of Events, *Sefer Toldot*, of his existence."[101]

This helps us understand two customs based on names:

- When a person is dangerously ill, a *shinui hashem*, change of name, is performed in the hope that this will change his destiny for the better.[102]

- We also have a custom that when a person has finished reciting the *Shemoneh Esrei*, he should recite a verse symbolizing his name, which begins and ends with the first and last letter of his Hebrew name. This, say the Sages, assures that this name will not be forgotten on the final day of judgment.

Let's dig a little deeper. The Rashba associates the concept of *shem*, name, with the idea of permanence.[103] A *shem* implies a lasting and meaningful status, which can be translated as reputation or fame. As the prophet Yeshayah tells us, the righteous will be granted a *yad*

---

101   *Koheles Rabbah* 7:3.
102   Rama, *Yoreh Deah* 335:10.
103   Rashba, Responsa 4:30.

vashem, position and permanence in G-d's House.[104] On the other hand, the *shem* or reputation of the wicked, says Shlomo HaMelech, is destined for erosion and disintegration.[105]

YOUR NAME IS WHERE YOU ARE

Let's take a slightly different look at how a name represents a person. The Ibn Ezra, in his *Sefer HaShem*, offers an etymological analysis. The word *shem* relates to the word *sham*, meaning "there," the word that describes the location of a given object. So a name locates its bearer in the sense that the combination of consonants and vowels that make a name serve as a substitute for the person. So when we say "David is wise," we are saying that the person who goes by that name, David, is wise.

Finally, the word *shem* has the same meaning as the word *shum*, meaning "assessment." The given name is in the nature of an estimation or assessment of the object or person it describes.

To add all this up, we have three understandings of the word *shem*:

1. Permanence
2. Location
3. Assessment

The thrust of them all is in the same direction. The idea of permanence attaches to that essence of the person's being that transcends the limitations of his physical being. The name represents the real person above and beyond his physical body. Even if the person is no longer in this world, his name lives on.

This is why, according to the Arizal, the name you are given is never a coincidence. As the *Amudei HaShamayim* explains, "Every name is a result of Divine intervention. Since it is clear to G-d what the essential nature and the activities of this person will be, the parents are inspired to name him in accordance with this. For the name explicitly relates to

---

104   *Yeshayah* 56:5.
105   *Mishlei* 10:7.

the essence and activities of this man, whether in the direction of good or the direction of bad."[106]

HOW MANY NAMES?

If we look through the Torah and Scriptures, we notice that many people are known by more than one name. The Ramban sets forth a rule that a person can be called by more than one name in Scripture, provided that both names have the same definition or basic meaning.[107] For example, in *Bereishis* one of Shimon's sons is named Tzochar,[108] and in *Bamidbar* it becomes Zerach.[109] Both however have the same meaning: something that shines brightly.

Sometimes a person will have different names depending on the context. The best known example of this is Yaakov's name. He was called *Yaakov*, which comes from the word for heel, *ekev*. This was because when he was born his hand was holding his twin brother Eisav's heel. Later in life, he was also called *Yisrael*, from *serarah*, to rule, because he triumphed over the angel.[110] So his early name connotes his lowly subservient nature, while the one given to him later in life implies strength and victory.

Finally, names can reflect the perception of the person who assigns them. The Midrash teaches that after Adam had given names to all the animals, G-d asked him, "Now what should your name be?" Adam answered, "I should be called 'Adam,' for I was formed from the earth." ['Adam' comes from *adamah*, earth.] G-d asked, "And what should My Name be?" Adam answered, "You should be called *Adon-ai*, for you are Master of everything." Surely, G-d did not need Adam to provide Him with His Name! Rather, G-d wanted Adam to spell out his own understanding of the nature of G-d and man.

---

106 This quote is from *Kuntres Krias HaShem*, included in *Sefer HaBris*, Rabbi Moshe Bunim Pirutinsky, New York, 5733.

107 *Bamidbar* 2:4.

108 *Bereishis* 46:10.

109 *Bamidbar* 26:13.

110 *Bereishis* 32:9.

With all of this information in mind, let's examine the four possible names the Talmud gives us for the Mashiach and see what we can glean from this information about the nature and mission of the Mashiach.

THE MASHIACH'S NAMES

Name One: Shiloh

The Talmud gives the first possible name of the Mashiach as Shiloh. It was actually the school of Rabbi Shela that gave him this name. This is a contraction of two words, *shai lo*, which means "a gift to him." This name is actually referenced in the Torah.[111] Before Yaakov died, he blessed each of his children. When Yaakov blessed Yehudah, he promised him that the kings of the Jewish people will emerge exclusively from among his tribe until the advent of the king Mashiach. The name Shiloh, says Yeshayah HaNavi, is a reference to the Mashiach on the basis of the verse, *"Yuval shai laHashem — A gift shall be offered to Hashem."*[112] This is because all the nations of the world will bring gifts to Israel and the Messianic king.

The *Daas Zekeinim* adds another interpretation of the name Shiloh: "In spite of many revolutions, exiles that will occur after the first king from the tribe of Yehudah, David, will ascend the throne, when the Mashiach who will be from the tribe of Yehudah will arrive, he will rule without anyone disputing his right to do so."[113] So Shiloh means permanent and unending kingship from David HaMelech to the Mashiach and beyond.

The name Shiloh has the same *gematria*, numerical value, as the name Moshe — both are 345 — because just as Moshe was the Mashiach of his time, Shiloh will be the redeemer at the time of the Mashiach.

Name Two: Yinon

The school of Yanai said the Mashiach's name will be Yinon. The word *Yinon* means "to continue" or "endure." This name is based upon the

---

111   Ibid. 49:10.
112   *Yeshayah* 18:7.
113   *Bereishis* 49:12.

Tehillim of David HaMelech, who prayed for the success of his descendant the Mashiach by saying, "May his name endure forever, for as long as the sun may his name continue." The word *yin* can also mean "fish," because when the Mashiach comes, the world will be fruitful and multiply just like the fish of the sea.

Name Three: Chaninah

The school of Chaninah said his name is Chaninah. This name is based on the words of Yirmiyah, "For I will not give you mercy."[114] The word *chen*, mercy, has the same root as the name Chaninah. The Mashiach will bring with him grace, peace, and harmony to the world.

Name Four: Menachem

The final opinion is that Menachem ben Chizkiyahu is his name. This is based on the verse, "A consolation to revive my spirit."[115] This is because he will come and be a *menachem*, a consolation, to his people who have suffered many years of pain and anguish from their exile and the destruction of the First and Second Temples.

The word Mashiach is made up of four letters, *mem*, *shin*, *yud*, and *ches*. The first letters of the four names described in the Talmud form an acronym and spell out the name Mashiach: **M**enachem, **S**hiloh, **Y**inon, **C**haninah.

One can't help but wonder how it can be that each school saw the name of the Mashiach to be almost exactly the same as the head of their institution. The Maharal of Prague points out a fascinating quality of the Mashiach — his character encompasses the virtue of every human being.[116] As each person studies the Mashiach, he will be drawn to seeing parts of his own personality in him.

According to the Maharal, then, these Sages are not actually disagreeing. Each one is simply stressing the aspect of the Mashiach's personality with which he is most familiar. For this reason, when these

---

114   *Yirmiyah* 16:13.
115   *Eichah* 1:16.
116   Maharal, *Netzach Yisrael* 41.

Sages attempted to determine the Mashiach's name (the name that best describes the Mashiach's personality), they determined it was the same as their own name!

Bar Nafli — Son of the Fallen One

The Talmud gives us another name of the future Mashiach; Bar Nafli, the descendant of the Fallen One.[117] Rabbi Nachman asked Rabbi Yitzchak, "Have you heard when Bar Nafli will come?" Rabbi Yitzchak asked, "Who is Bar Nafli?" Rabbi Nachman responded, "The Mashiach." "You call him Bar Nafli?" asked Rabbi Yitzchak. "Yes, as the prophet Amos describes the Future Redemption in the following way, 'On that day I will raise up the fallen booth of David, *succas David hanofeles*, I will repair their breaches and raise up its ruins, and I will raise it up as in days of old.'"[118] The word *hanofeles*, the fallen one, is related to the name Bar Nafli, the son of the fallen one.

Rashi explains that by giving the name Bar Nafli, son of the fallen kingdom of David, Rabbi Nachman is informing us that this name reflects the mission of the Mashiach to reestablish the fallen Davidic dynasty.[119] The Mashiach will not be building a new dynasty but he will restore that which is currently fallen. For this reason, the verse in Amos refers to the monarchy of David as a *succah*, booth, rather than a *bayis*, house, which is the more common term for a royal dynasty. When a house collapses, the structure is typically ruined and an entirely new one must be built in its stead. But when a booth collapses, the entire structure is easily restored to its former state. This is why the Rambam writes, "The Messianic king will arise and restore the monarchy of David to its former state, to its original dominion."[120]

The *Ben Yehoyada* on this piece of Talmud says that this is hinted at by the *gematria*, numerical value, of the words Bar Nafli and Ben Yishai, the son of Yishai (i.e., David); both are 372.

---

117   *Sanhedrin* 96b–97a.
118   *Amos* 9:11.
119   Rashi, *Sanhedrin* 97a.
120   Rambam, *Mishneh Torah, Melachim* 11:1.

THE PERSONAL QUALITIES OF THE MASHIACH

We already spoke about how the Mashiach will be great in a number of ways, with a level of prophecy second only to Moshe Rabbeinu, and wisdom superior to the "wisest of all men," Shlomo HaMelech.

The Rambam describes the Mashiach as a normal person of flesh and blood, of humble background. As the Rambam says, "He will not be a known person that can be identified beforehand as the son of so-and-so from such-and-such family."[121] This means that his qualification as the Mashiach is not dependent on his family's status among the people. What will qualify him are his personal qualities and the signs and wonders he will perform, which will act as a proof that he is the true Mashiach. This is very much in line with the prophet Yeshayah's words when he says, "For he shot up like a sapling, like a root out of dry ground."[122] He will arrive without anyone knowing anything about his father, mother, or family.

The prophet Yeshayah outlines six personal qualities of the Mashiach.[123] Each of these qualities is a key ingredient to understanding him and his eventual role for mankind.

> *And the spirit of Hashem will rest upon him, a spirit of wisdom and understanding, a spirit of counsel and strength, a spirit of knowledge and fear of the Hashem.*

The use of the expression "rest upon him," *nachah alav*, means that the following traits have permanence and aren't just fleeting abilities. His greatness will have permanence. Let's examine each of these six traits:

1. *Ruach Chachmah* — **A Spirit of Wisdom**: This refers to having great knowledge, which he will have amassed though many years of study. He will have retained this knowledge and be able to recall it.

---

121   Rambam, *Iggeres Teiman*, pg. 56.
122   *Yeshayah* 53:2.
123   Ibid. 11:2–3.

2. *Ruach Binah* — **A Spirit of Understanding:** This means that he will have the ability not only to amass knowledge but to use that knowledge to deduce more important ideas and know how to apply this wisdom. In today's language he could be called book smart, yet at the same time street smart, and able to use and convey the information he knows.

3. *Ruach Eitzah* — **A Spirit of Counsel:** While the Mashiach will be book smart, he also will have the ability to counsel people and have an incredible ability to work with people and understand human nature.

4. *Ruach Gevurah* — **A Spirit of Strength:** He will have the strength of character to face all difficulties as they arise, making decisions fairly and with great courage.

5. *Ruach Daas* — **A Spirit of Knowledge:** The Mashiach will use his knowledge to obtain a real understanding of G-d and to be a true servant of G-d.

6. *Ruach Yiras Hashem* — **A Spirit of Fear of Hashem:** All his knowledge and wisdom will culminate with a truly spiritual and holy man who will fear G-d in all his actions.

Each of these six personal traits possessed by the Mashiach will be cultivated by him over the course of his life. He will use each of them to further his mission of bringing ultimate peace to the world. If even one of them is missing, his entire mission and its success will be compromised. Having wisdom is important, but being able to use that wisdom in arriving at important decisions is equally important. Conveying that information to people in order to guide and lead them, while at the same time standing strong and showing your convictions, are crucial leadership qualities. Doing all this, while being dedicated to the knowledge of G-d and being fearful of G-d in all his actions, is key to fulfilling the mission of being the Mashiach.

Chapter Eight

YECHEZKEL AND THE VALLEY OF DRY BONES

WHEN DESCRIBING THE state of the Jewish people before the Mashiach comes, one of the most graphic depictions can be found in the prophet Yechezkel's vision of the valley of dry bones. In it, Yechezkel describes a pile of dry bones that lay lifeless in the midst of a valley. Miraculously, Yechezkel is able to bring these bones back to fresh and vigorous life.[124] Let's take a deeper look at the words of Yechezkel and see what this vision can reveal to us about the End of Days:

The Hand of the Lord came upon me, and carried me out in the Spirit of the Lord, and set me down in the midst of the valley that was full of bones. And He made me pass by them round about, and lo! they were exceedingly many on the surface of the valley, and lo! they were exceedingly dry. Then He said to me, "Son of man, can these bones become alive?" And I answered, "O Lord G-d, You alone know."

And He said to me, "Prophesy over these bones, and say to them, 'O dry bones, hear the word of the Lord. So says the Lord G-d to these bones: Behold, I will cause spirit to enter into you, and you shall live!

---

124 *Yechezkel* 37:1–14.

"'And I will lay sinews upon you, and I will make flesh grow over you and cover you with skin and put breath into you, and you will live, and you will then know that I am the Lord.'" So I prophesied as I was commanded, and there arose a noise when I prophesied, and behold a commotion, and the bones came together, bone to its bone!

And I looked, and lo! sinews were upon them, and flesh came upon them, and skin covered them from above, but there was still no spirit in them. Then He said to me, "Prophesy to the spirit, prophesy, O son of man, and say to the spirit, 'So says the Lord G-d: From four sides come, O spirit, and breathe into these slain ones that they may live.'"

And I prophesied as He had commanded me, and the spirit came into them, and they lived and stood on their feet, a very great army, exceedingly so.

Then He said to me, "Son of man, these bones are all the House of Israel. Behold they say, 'Our bones have become dried up, our hope is lost, we are doomed!'

"Therefore, prophesy and say to them, 'So says the Lord G-d: Lo! I open your graves and cause you to come up out of your graves as My people, and bring you home to the Land of Israel.

"'Then you shall know that I am the Lord, when I open your graves and lead you up out of your graves as My people. And I will put My spirit into you, and you shall live, and I will set you on your land, and you shall know that I, the Lord, have spoken it and have performed it, says the Lord.'"

Who are these dry bones and when will they be resurrected? The Ramban says that the awakening of these dry bones is not referring to the resurrection of the dead at the End of Days, but rather to the Messianic Redemption.[125]

---

125   *Bereishis* 18:25, 24:3, and *Devarim* 11:18.

Who then exactly are the dry bones? They represent us, the Jewish people in exile. We are like a collection of dry bones. We are dead like a corpse numb to all the events swirling around us. The Final Redemption is compared to resurrection in that we will be brought back to life.

The resurrection described by the prophet is not meant to be taken literally, but instead refers to a spiritual rejuvenation so striking that it is compared to an actual resuscitation.

> The Jewish people in exile are like a collection of dry bones.

THE KING OF KHAZAR

In his work *Kuzari*, Rabbi Yehudah HaLevi has the king of Khazar ask questions to a Christian priest, Muslim Imam, and Jewish rabbi to discover the one true religion. In one of his answers, the rabbi compares the Jewish people in exile to scattered bones. Responding to the Khazar king's comments that without prophets and priests the Jewish people are like a body without a head and heart, the rabbi says the following:

> *What you say is true! Moreover, we have no real bones, just scattered bones, akin to the bones Yechezkel saw in his vision. Nevertheless, King of Khazar, these bones have some remnant of life in them for they once were utensils for the head, heart, life force, spirit, and soul. They therefore are better than the intact bodies whose head, eyes, ears, and remaining parts are made of stone and plaster. These bodies never had the spirit of life rest within them, nor is it possible that they ever will. Rather, they are forms that resemble man, but are not really man...*[126]

Although we have been without prophets and have been exiled from our land for over two thousand years, the Jewish people are still alive. We have through the centuries resembled a sack of bones, but these

---

126   *Kuzari, Maamar 2.*

bones will once again be covered in flesh and new life will spring forth from them. Very much like the survivors of the Holocaust who were reduced to nothingness after the war, losing their families, homes, and everything else, they were still able to recreate their lives and put flesh back onto their bones, reviving their lives and breathing back life into their shattered existence.

Chapter Nine

THE MASHIACH AND HIS PROPHETIC SENSE OF SMELL

PEOPLE CLAIMING TO be the Mashiach is nothing new. Since we don't know who the actual Mashiach will be until he reveals himself to us, this has left room for many people over the centuries to falsely claim they are the Mashiach. It is clear all candidates from the past were not the Mashiach; by looking at the list of duties and roles the Mashiach has — including world peace, rebuilding of the Third Temple in Yerushalayim, and so on — it is pretty obvious that the Mashiach has not yet arrived, although we are definitely close.

Jewish history has been replete with people claiming themselves to be the Mashiach or others claiming such about them. Much blood has been spilled because of these unscrupulous individuals or because of their handlers or promoters. Such claims have been made for thousands of years. The Talmud discusses one of them — about an individual by the name of Bar Kochba.

Before we look into his story, let's try to understand one of the credentials the Mashiach must have in order to be considered the long-awaited redeemer: his incredible prophetic sense of smell.

SMELLING IS BELIEVING

We already mentioned that the Mashiach will be a great prophet, second only to Moshe Rabbeinu. The prophet Yeshayah makes the following statement about the Mashiach's prophetic ability: "And he shall be imbued by the fear of Hashem, and will not need to judge by what his eyes see, nor decide by what his ears hear."[127] The Hebrew word for "imbued" is *vaharicho*. The Talmud identifies the similarity between *vaharicho*, and another Hebrew word: *rei'ach*, smell. "Rava said: He will smell a person and judge him."[128] What does the Mashiach judging by his sense of smell mean?

The Mashiach will be imbued with a prophetic sense of smell enabling him to have a lightning-like intuitive grasp of what is right and what is not. This will come through his imbued sense of smell and not his logical understanding of what he hears or sees.

Of all the senses we humans possess (touching, seeing, hearing, and tasting), smelling is considered the most spiritual. Let's explore why this should be. When Adam and Chava were in the Garden of Eden, they gave in to their desires and ate from the *Eitz HaDaas*, the Tree of Knowledge. G-d permitted them to eat from all the delicious fruits and every tree in the Garden, however they were told to not eat from one tree, and that was the *Eitz HaDaas*. Soon after, they were both tempted to eat. Before they did so, however, they first saw (seeing) the fruit, then they touched (touching) the tree, and finally they ate (tasting) from the tree after hearing (hearing) G-d tell them not to eat from it. The only thing they didn't do was smell the fruit.

Since they never used their sense of smell in this first sin, the Kabbalists tell us that the sense of smell has never been negatively affected, and therefore is the purest of all the five senses — and probably the most sensitive.

> The sense of smell has never been negatively affected, and therefore is the purest of all the five senses.

So powerful is this sense of smell that the rabbis actually used this ability as a way to determine if someone actually was the awaited Mashiach. His name was Bar Kochba.

---

127   *Yeshayah* 11:3.
128   *Sanhedrin* 93b.

BAR KOCHBA — THE UNSUCCESSFUL MASHIACH

Jewish history has been replete with people claiming they are the chosen Mashiach. One of these unsuccessful Mashiachs came about in the Talmudic era. His name was Shimon Bar Kochba, or as the Talmud refers to him, Bar Koziva. He was the Jewish king who revolted against Rome under the Emperor Hadrian after the destruction of the Second Temple, and whom Rabbi Akiva and other Sages felt could be the Mashiach. After ruling for two and a half years, Shimon Bar Kochba declared he was the Mashiach. The Sages tested him and asked, "It is said of the Mashiach that he has the power to judge through smelling, if you have the power to smell and judge you are the Mashiach. Let us test you to see if you can smell and judge." When they realized he wasn't imbued with this ability, they realized that he was not the Mashiach and the Jews deserted him. The Romans became very distrustful of Bar Kochba after this and killed him soon after.[129]

DIVIDING THE LAND INTO ITS TRIBES

The Mashiach will utilize this perfect sense of smell to determine information which logic could not dictate. An example of this is that the Mashiach will be able to determine a person's tribal affiliation. For example, a person may not realize it, but he may actually be a *Kohen* and therefore fit to serve in the Temple in Yerushalayim. If he is unaware of his ancestry, he wouldn't know that he has this important role to play in the Temple. The Mashiach, using his prophetic sense of smell, will reveal to that person his illustrious heritage that connects him to his direct ancestor Aaron, the older brother of Moshe Rabbeinu. He will begin with the tribe of Levi, determining the legitimacy of each *Kohen* and *Levi*.

This purification of the *Kohanim* and *Levi'im* is what the prophet Malachi was referring to when he said that the Mashiach will "purify the children of Levi, and refine them like gold and silver, to become

---

129   Ibid.

bearers of an offering to G-d in righteousness."[130] After this purification, the *Kohanim* will once again strictly observe the laws of the sacrificial service.

After determining from which tribe every Jew originates, the Mashiach will use this information to divide the Land of Israel into land inheritances, with each tribe receiving its proper portion. After the Jewish people entered the Land of Israel in the time of Yehoshua, the Land was conquered for a period of seven years, following which it was divided into its tribal affiliations, which took another seven years in total. We are not sure how long the future dividing of the Land will take, but each tribe will once again take its ancestral land, as they once did before.

What we need to examine now is to what degree the Messianic era will be a time of miracles.

THE MESSIANIC ERA — MIRACULOUS OR MUNDANE

Two great scholars, Shmuel and Rabbi Yochanan, discuss how miraculous existence in the Messianic era will be:

- According to Shmuel, the only difference between the world we see now and when the Mashiach will be here is that the Jewish people will be free at last from the subjugation of foreign nations who have attempted to destroy, exile, and hold dominion over us for thousands of years.[131] The proof Shmuel brings for this is based upon the verse in *Devarim* that "poor people will not cease to exist within the land."[132] So according to Shmuel, the natural laws and even the basic norms of society will not change in the Messianic era.
- Rabbi Yochanan disagrees and sees the time that the Mashiach finally rules over us to be a time of revealed miracles and the suspension of natural laws.[133] The proof Rabbi Yochanan brings for this is based on the words of Yeshayah HaNavi: "And

---

130   *Malachi* 3:3.
131   *Sanhedrin* 99a and *Berachos* 34b.
132   *Devarim* 15:11.
133   *Bava Basra* 75a.

I will make your windows of rubies, and your gates of beryl, and all your borders of precious stones."[134] Rabbi Yochanan expounded on these words by saying, "The Holy One, Blessed Be He, is destined to bring precious stones and pearls that are thirty-by-thirty (cubits) and hollow out of them an area ten-by-twenty and stand them at the gates of Yerushalayim."[135] He saw all the incredible prophecies that are spoken of in Scriptures apply to the Messianic period and not the World to Come, which is the period following the resurrection of the dead.

The Rambam seems to side with the opinion of Shmuel. In the words of the Rambam: "Do not think that in the Messianic era any of the current norms will cease or that there will be a change in the natural order. Rather the world will function in its normal manner. That which is said by Yeshayah — 'The wolf will live with the sheep and the leopard will lie down with the kid; and a calf, a lion cub and a falling will walk together, and a young child will lead them'[136] — is merely a metaphor whose point is that the Jewish people will live securely with the other nations who had wanted to harm them…those nations will not steal or destroy and they will live in harmony with Israel."[137]

However, the Rambam gives a slightly different opinion when he writes, "A human being does not have the capacity to properly comprehend the goodness of the World to Come. No one knows its glory, beauty, and potency except for G-d Himself. All the benefits predicted for Israel are only physical matters, which the Jewish people will enjoy in the Messianic era when their sovereignty is restored. The goodness of the life in the World to Come is immeasurable and utterly beyond comparison."[138]

The Rambam is apparently citing the view of both Shmuel and Rabbi Yochanan. But Shmuel and Rabbi Yochanan are disagreeing with each

---

134   *Yeshayah* 54:12.
135   *Bava Basra* 75a.
136   *Yeshayah* 11:6.
137   Rambam, *Mishneh Torah, Melachim* 12:1–2; *Teshuvah* 9:2.
138   Ibid., *Teshuvah* 8:7.

other! The *Lechem Mishnah* answers this apparent contradiction by suggesting that Rabbi Yochanan agrees that the natural laws will not change. Rabbi Yochanan's point of contention with Shmuel is that he maintains that human society will rise to a utopian level of peace and cooperation, whereas Shmuel holds that the current norms of society will continue (as is evidenced by Shmuel's proof text of "poor people will not cease to exist").[139]

According to this approach, the Rambam's rulings are entirely consistent with Rabbi Yochanan's view. When the Rambam cited Shmuel's words, "There is no difference between the Present World and the Messianic era except for foreign dominion,"[140] he did so only to support his point that the laws of nature will remain in effect and not because he adopts the view of Shmuel.

MASHIACH — THE EIGHTH ERA

Mashiach is best represented by the number eight. In order to appreciate the number eight and its connection to Mashiach, we need to examine the number that precedes it: the number seven. The number seven represents the physical world we live in now. The world was created in six days and G-d rested on the seventh. So we count the days of the week from one to seven, then revert back to one again.

These seven days are referred to as the "Seven Pillars of Creation."[141] The completion of the world in seven days parallels the seven primary *Sefiros*,[142] Divine Emanations, to embrace the whole natural realm. The natural world is said to encompass seven deserts, seven lands,[143] seven rivers, seven seas,[144] and seven mountains.[145] The seven days of creation were also reflected in the seven branches of the Menorah, with the

---

139   Ibid. 9:2.
140   Ibid.; *Melachim* 12:2.
141   *Sanhedrin* 38a, interpreting *Mishlei* 9:1.
142   These seven *Sefiros* are based upon the verses in *Divrei HaYamim I* 29:11–12.
143   *Midrash Tehillim* 92:2.
144   *Pirkei d'Rebbi Eliezer* 12.
145   Ibid. 18.

middle branch symbolic of Shabbos.[146] The number seven is also seen within the personal passage of man's life as it unfolds in seven distinct phases.[147] The number seven therefore represents "the Present World."

The foundation of the Jewish people was also built upon the number seven. The ancestors of the *Bnei Yisrael* were the three Patriarchs (Avraham, Yitzchak, and Yaakov) and four Matriarchs (Sarah, Rivkah, Rachel, and Leah). Together they make up the seven holy ancestors of the Jewish people. In addition, there were seven generations from Avraham to Moshe Rabbeinu until *Matan Torah* at Har Sinai.[148]

In terms of leadership, there were seven holy "Shepherds of Israel."[149] We also have seven prophetesses whose prophecies were recorded for the Jewish people.[150] Seven great individuals, *Ushpizin*, guests, are associated with visiting during the seven days of Succos.[151]

The number eight follows the number seven and therefore represents that which is *above* the physical world: the spiritual realm. In Jewish thought, the number eight represents the transcendent spiritual world that resides above the natural world. This is why a Jewish baby is circumcised and becomes fully part of the Jewish people on the eighth day. On Chanukah, the lights miraculously lasted for eight days.

The miraculous oil of Chanukah is a harbinger of the anointing oil used to inaugurate the coming of the Messianic era. This process can be traced to David HaMelech, who was the eighth of Yishai's sons.

The Messianic epoch is intrinsically linked to the number eight — a metaphysical number for a metaphysical period of history. The Talmud

---

146 R' Tzadok HaKohen, *Pri Tzaddik*, BeHa'aloscha 3.

147 The seven phases unfold as follows: (1) a king (a newborn until one-year-old treated regally), (2) pig (two-year-old toddler rolling in dirt), (3) kid (five-year-old dancing before his mother), (4) horse (eighteen-year-old youth proudly running with vigor), (5) donkey (forty-year-old heavily laden with the yoke of parenthood), (6) dog (impudence with little shame), (7) monkey (old age). *Tanchumah*, *Pekudei* 3.

148 *Yalkut Shemoni*, *Shemos* 19:276.

149 *Sukkah* 52b. They are identified as Adam, Sheis, Mesushelach, Avraham, Yaakov, Moshe, and David.

150 *Megillah* 14a. They are Sarah, Miriam, Devorah, Chana, Avigayil, Chuldah, and Esther.

151 *Zohar* 3, 103b. They are Avraham, Yitzchak, Yaakov, Moshe, Aaron, Yosef, and David.

tells us that "in the year after the seventh, the Mashiach will come."[152] The harp used both by the *Levi'im* in the Temple and by David HaMelech to sing praises to Hashem had seven strings; the harp in the era of the Mashiach will have eight strings.[153] This symbolically represents the higher eighth dimension of the Messianic era, which will be exalted over the non-miraculous world we live in today. In other words, the Messianic era will literally be out of this world!

---

152   *Sanhedrin* 97a.
153   *Erachin* 13b.

Chapter Ten

THE RETURN TO THE LAND OF ISRAEL

ONE OF THE signs before the advent of the Messianic era is that the Land of Israel will blossom and give out the most incredible fruits after a long period of desolation. This is based on the prophecy of Yechezkel in which he says, "But you, O mountains of Israel, will give forth your branch and bear your fruit for My people Israel, for they are soon to come."[154] When the Jewish people were driven from the Land following the destruction of the Second Temple, it wasn't just the people who suffered; the Land itself did as well and became a barren desert. This carried on for hundreds of years. What was once a fertile land full of fruits and vegetables soon became an inhospitable land incapable of bringing out much more than weeds.

According to Rav Abba in the Talmud, there is no clearer indication of the imminent arrival of the Mashiach than the Land of Israel resuming its production of fruit in preparation for the return of the Jewish people.[155] The Maharsha explains that when Israel is not inhabited by the Jewish people, the Land does not produce fruit to its usual degree. Thus, when it resumes producing fruit, this is a clear sign that the time is approaching for the Jewish people's return to their land.[156]

---

154 *Yechezkel* 36:8.

155 *Sanhedrin* 98a.

156 Maharsha, *Sanhedrin* ibid.

The increase in agricultural activity will seem almost miraculous. Yeshayah HaNavi speaks of water sources opening up in unlikely locations: "I will open up rivers upon the hilltops and springs in the midst of valleys; I will turn the desert into a pond of water and a parched land into sources of water. I will plant in the wilderness cedar, acacia, myrtle, and pine tree; I will set cypress, fir, and boxwood together in the desert."[157] Generally speaking, hilltops and deserts are not places we generally find water.

These verses are to be understood literally, i.e., that the Land will produce fruits in the most unlikely of locations. According to some, these miracles are also metaphors depicting the transformation of Israel from a wretched band of exiles into a thriving vibrant community. Very much like the Jews who arrived in Israel during the First and Second Aliyot and after the Holocaust, with little more than the shirts on their backs, they created a vibrant state that seems almost impossible to understand without Divine intervention.

If you think that Israel has always looked lush and green, we have an account from Mark Twain who visited Israel in 1867 describing the Land of Israel like this, in his book *Innocents Abroad*:

> *We traversed some miles of desolate country whose soil is rich enough but is given wholly to weeds — a silent, mournful expanse...A desolation is here that not even imagination can grace with the pomp of life and action. We reached Tabor safely... We never saw a human being on the whole route. We pressed on toward the goal of our crusade, renowned Jerusalem. The further we went, the hotter the sun got and the more rocky and bare, repulsive and dreary the landscape became... There was hardly a tree or a shrub anywhere. Even the olive and the cactus, those fast friends of a worthless soil, had almost deserted the country. No landscape exists that is more tiresome to the eye than that which bounds the approaches to Jerusalem...Jerusalem is*

---

157   *Yeshayah* 41:18–19.

> *mournful, dreary and lifeless. I would not desire to live here.
> It is a hopeless, dreary, heartbroken land... Palestine sits in
> sackcloth and ashes.*[158]

This doesn't sound too much like the Israel we know today with its fine fruits and vegetables.

THE BLOOMING OF THE LAND

What is the purpose of the agricultural success of the Land and its connection to the coming of the Mashiach? Two possible answers are given to this question. They both come from the Radak in his commentary to *Yeshayah*:[159]

- The first is a practical answer. When the Jews return to Israel to build up the Land, they'll be working out in the fields, preparing the land for cultivation and for building. The Israeli heat can be oppressive, especially during the summer months, so G-d preempted their arrival with trees so they could find shade from the sun.
- His second answer has more global implications. When the world sees and hears about the incredible advancements that the Jews have had by turning a desert into a lush paradise, they will be amazed, and even they will realize that something incredible is happening in the holy Land of Israel, created by G-d on behalf of the Jewish people.

This is hinted at in the order of the *Amidah* prayer that we say three times a day. The Talmud asks why the Sages instituted saying the blessing for the ingathering of the exiles in the silent *Amidah* after the blessing for bountiful years.[160] There it answers that this order of events is hinted at in the verse, "But You, O mountains of Israel, will give forth

---

158 Mark Twain, *Innocents Abroad* (American Publishing Company, 1869), chaps. 54–55, www.gutenberg.org/files/3176/3176-h/3176-h.htm.

159 Radak, *Yeshayah* 41:18–19.

160 *Megillah* 17b.

your branch and bear your fruit for My people Israel, for they are soon to come."[161] Rashi adds that this implies the ingathering of the exiles will happen at a time of bountiful harvests.

FROM YERUSHALAYIM THE SPIRITUAL LIGHT WILL SHINE OUT

As the Mashiach's powers develop, so will his fame. Not only will the Jewish people seek out the Mashiach for advice and guidance, but many non-Jews will recognize his profound wisdom and come to seek his advice. Among his many areas of instruction, the Mashiach will teach people how to live in peace and follow G-d's laws. They will stream to Yerushalayim, as the prophet Michah said: "It will be in the End of Days that the mountain of the Temple of Hashem will be firmly established as the most prominent of the mountains, and it will be exalted up above the hills, and peoples will stream to it. Many nations will go and say, 'Come let us go up to the mountain of Hashem and to the Temple of the G-d of Yaakov, and He will teach us of His ways and we will walk in His paths.' For from Zion shall go forth the Torah, and the word of Hashem from Yerushalayim."[162]

As the fame and power of the Mashiach grows, so will his spiritual influence shine throughout the world. The nations of the world will travel swiftly toward the spiritual light that streams forth from the Temple.

Even Winston Churchill understood the eternal connection between Yerushalayim and the Jewish people. When talking to an official after taking office as prime minister again in 1951, he remarked, "You ought to let the Jews have Jerusalem — it was they who made it famous."[163] This may explain why Yerushalayim in our day has grown so rapidly into the physical and spiritual home to so many Jews. Yerushalayim was a city never given its due respect when controlled by the Jordanians or the many other nations that have occupied it before then. This changed when Israel regained control over the Holy City in 1967. Since then

---

161 *Yechezkel* 36:8.

162 *Michah* 4:1–2.

163 Simon Sebag Montefiore, *Jerusalem — An Autobiography* (Vintage Books, 2011), pg. 507.

we have seen it flourish and grow in the most remarkable way as the Jewish capital of Israel and the Jewish people.

It will be because of these teachings that the prophecy of Michah will come true: "He will judge between many peoples, and will settle the arguments of mighty nations from far away. They will beat their swords into plowshares and their spears into pruning hooks; nation will not lift sword against nation, nor will they learn war anymore."

CONVERTS JOIN THE JEWISH PEOPLE

As we have seen, the Mashiach is the redeemer for all people, not just the Jewish people. Although in Messianic times, the falsehood of other religions will become readily apparent, that does not mean that these nations and their people will become Jewish. They don't need to become Jewish in order to have a connection to the G-d of Israel. Still, right before and during the early stages of the Messianic era, as the drama begins to unfold, many gentiles will feel compelled to convert to Judaism. This may explain the many converts we have seen in our generation joining the ranks of the Jewish people. This will continue until at some point converts will no longer be accepted. This will happen once the Mashiach has revealed himself. Why will the door to conversion be closed once the Mashiach reveals himself?

> Right before and during the early stages of the Messianic era, many gentiles will feel compelled to convert to Judaism.

The answer is that conversion to Judaism is reserved for those gentiles who truly wish to convert for authentic reasons. The Talmud explains further and says that once the Mashiach comes, Israel will then be ascendant and it can be assumed that would-be-converts will be acting out of ulterior motives.[164] This was actually the case in the times of David HaMelech and Shlomo HaMelech, when the sages at these times prevented gentiles from converting. In the time of David HaMelech, they were concerned that gentiles were converting out of fear, and in

---

164   *Avodah Zarah* 3b.

the time of Shlomo HaMelech they had the opposite concern — that gentiles would want to join the Jewish people because of the Jewish people's prosperity and preeminence.

THE ROLE OF THE NON-JEWISH NATIONS BEFORE THE MASHIACH COMES

We have seen the role that the Jewish people need to play in order to expedite the arrival of the Mashiach. What is the role of the non-Jewish nations? What part do they need to play in order to allow them to be worthy of redemption?

Jews were given 613 mitzvos. These laws enable us to fulfill our spiritual mission in this world. Do the other nations also have mitzvos that enable them to bring blessing and success into their lives?

The answer is absolutely yes! When G-d created Adam and Chava, He gave them six laws that all humanity was to abide by. After the flood of Noah, these six laws were joined by another one to create a total of seven laws.[165]

The seven laws are referred to as the *Sheva Mitzvos l'Bnei Noach*, the Seven Laws of Noah. Noah was a righteous individual who was tasked with rebuilding the world after the Flood wiped humanity away. In doing so, he earned inclusion in the title for the seven laws that were given to bring perfection to mankind. These laws have applied since those days until current times. They are found in various places in the Torah and carry great weight when heavenly judgment is brought against non-Jewish nations to ascertain whether they have been fulfilling their mission in this world.

Let's examine these Seven Laws of Noah to understand how non-Jews can earn a part in the Messianic Redemption.

Law One: All nations must create a fair and just law court system.

According to the Rambam, this requires Noahites to establish courts to enforce the other six commandments.[166] How must the gentiles fulfill

---

165   The prohibition against eating flesh from a living animal was added in Noah's time, as *Bereishis* 9:4 states: "Nevertheless, you may not eat flesh with its life, which is its blood."

166   Rambam, *Mishneh Torah*, *Melachim* 9:14.

the commandment to establish laws and courts? They are obligated to set up judges and magistrates in every major city to render judgment concerning these six mitzvos and to admonish the people regarding their observance.

The Ramban adds that this commandment requires Noahites not only to establish courts, but to observe a system of civil law, such as with regard to theft, fraud, wages, damages, bodily injuries, loans, sales, and commercial dealings.[167]

Law Two: "Blessing" the Divine Name

The word blessing over here is used as a euphemism. The command forbids cursing the Name of G-d.

Law Three: No Idolatry

The Noahites are not permitted to worship any god other than the true One G-d.

Law Four: No Forbidden Sexual Relationships

There are six illicit sexual relations forbidden to a gentile:[168]

    A. His mother
    B. His father's wife, even though she is not his mother
    C. A woman married to somebody else
    D. His maternal sister
    E. A male to a male
    F. An animal

These prohibitions are derived from the verse in *Bereishis*: "Therefore, a man shall leave his father and his mother and cling to his wife and they shall become one flesh."[169] The words "one flesh" mean that intimate relationships are only to be built with those outside of the six groups listed above.

---

167   Ramban, *Bereishis* 34:13.
168   Rambam, *Mishneh Torah, Melachim* 9:5.
169   *Bereishis* 2:24.

Law Five: No Murder

Noahites are forbidden to take another person's life.

Law Six: No Stealing

A gentile is liable for violating the prohibition against theft, whether he stole from another gentile or from a Jew.

This applies to one who forcefully robs an individual or steals money, a kidnapper, an employer who withholds his worker's wages and the like, even a worker who eats from his employer's produce when he is not working. In all such cases, he is liable and is considered as a robber.[170]

Law Seven: No Eating the Limb of a Live Animal

Eating a limb that was ripped from an animal when it was still alive is forbidden to all Noahites.

The Rambam adds a caveat for a Noahite who is following these laws:

> *Anyone who accepts upon himself the fulfillment of these seven mitzvos and is precise in their observance is considered one of "the pious among the gentiles" and will merit a share in the World to Come.*
>
> *This applies only when he accepts them and fulfills them because the Holy One, Blessed Be He, commanded them in the Torah and informed us through Moshe Rabbeinu that Noah's descendants had been commanded to fulfill them previously.*
>
> *However, if he fulfills them out of intellectual conviction, he is not a resident alien, nor of "the pious among the gentiles," but of "their wise men."[171]*

---

170   Rambam, *Mishneh Torah, Melachim* 9:9.
171   Ibid. 8:11.

IF OUR ANCESTORS COULDN'T BRING THE MASHIACH, WHAT CHANCE DO WE HAVE?

Looking back through Jewish history, we have been blessed with incredible men and women who have achieved great things for our people, the Land of Israel, and the entire world — from Avraham and Sarah, through the centuries of the great prophets and prophetesses, right up to the present day. The question that needs to be answered is this: If the great people of previous generations didn't merit bringing the Mashiach, what chance do we have of bringing him?

It's a fair question. We have seen what is called in Jewish thought a *yeridas hadoros*, the diminishing spiritual level of subsequent generations. From the time of Adam and Chava, who were created directly by G-d, each subsequent generation has been a little diminished from those perfect spiritual beings. Much like a photocopy that becomes less and less clear the further you are from the original, so too, each generation is further away from the original.

If Avraham and Sarah couldn't merit the Mashiach, and neither could Moshe Rabbeinu, Aaron, Miriam, all the prophets, Mordechai and Esther, Ezra, Rashi, the Rambam, the Ramban, until Rabbi Moshe Feinstein, and tens of thousands like them, what chance do we have?

To answer this question, let's use a metaphor that we are all aware of: the Western Wall in Yerushalayim. If you've seen the Western Wall, you may have realized that the part of the Wall you look at when you're standing on the plaza is only a small part of the original. When you travel down into the tunnels under the Western Wall, known as the Kosel Tunnels, the wall continues below the surface. The stones at the base of the wall are incredibly large, some of them weighing many tons. The further you look up at the wall, the smaller the stones get until you reach the very top of the wall where the stones are so small you could hold each one in your hands.

Each generation cannot be looked at in isolation. We can't evaluate each generation's merit, but the sum total of all the generations. There is a cumulative effect whereby each generation builds on the one that precedes it. We aren't alone in history, and each generation's merit isn't sufficient to bring the Mashiach. But when we add every great person and every previous generation, the merit accumulates, and we are able to bring the Mashiach.

Chapter Eleven

YERUSHALAYIM — THE SPIRITUAL METROPOLIS OF THE WORLD

IF YOU'VE EVER been to Yerushalayim and spent even a short time at the Kosel, the Western Wall, you have sensed a small feeling of what the world will be like once the Third Temple is reestablished on the Temple Mount. Jews and non-Jews come from all four corners of the earth to feel the connection to the One Living G-d, His Land, and His people when they stand next to those large and silent stones.

We have already noted that one of the jobs of the Mashiach will be to rebuild the Third Temple. Actually, as we already read in the Rambam, the Mashiach will have to actually build the Temple in Yerushalayim in order to prove he is the one true Mashiach. The Mashiach's first appearance, says the Rambam, will be in the Land of Israel.[172] This is what the last prophet Malachi meant when he said, "Suddenly, he will come to His Temple."

The prophet Yeshayah already told us how Yerushalayim will be at the center of all the action before and after the Mashiach arrives: "The mountain of the Temple of G-d will be firmly established as the head of the mountains, and it will be exalted above the hills…"[173] This is a

---

172   Rambam, *Iggeres Teiman*, pp. 55–56.
173   *Yeshayah* 2:2.

reference to Har HaMoriah, the future home of the Third and final Temple in Yerushalayim. This mountain was where Avraham brought his son Yitzchak as a potential sacrifice to G-d, and the same mountain Avraham's grandson Yaakov spent the night on his way out of Israel when escaping from his twin brother Eisav, where he slept and dreamt of a ladder from the earth to the heavens — the famous vision of "Yaakov's ladder."

The prophet is telling us that this mountain is different from all other hills and mountains the world over. Throughout history, people have worshipped their idols and false gods upon high mountains and hills, however, once the Mashiach comes, only one mountain will have any status in the world as a place of worship and spiritual growth, and that is Har HaMoriah, the mountain of G-d.

Rashi, in his commentary to this verse, points out that metaphorically speaking, "mountains and hills" always represent great miracles that took place on high mountains throughout Jewish history. These include: when we were standing at Mount Sinai, a humble mountain in the Sinai desert where the Jewish people stood ready to receive the Torah forty-nine days after leaving Egypt; on Mount Carmel, where the prophet Eliyahu proved G-d's word to be true after defeating a horde of idolaters who attempted to sacrifice to their god unsuccessfully; and also on Mount Tabor, where the Jewish armies defeated the powerful army of Sisera. Each of these miracles and the mountains they took place on will pale into insignificance compared to the Temple Mount in Yerushalayim after the Mashiach appears.

YERUSHALAYIM WON'T HAVE ENOUGH ROOM

In preparation for the return of the Jewish people to the holy city of Yerushalayim, the prophets speak about one of the precursors to the arrival of the Mashiach: the rebuilding and population burst inside Yerushalayim. David HaMelech says, "The builder of Yerushalayim is G-d, the outcast of Israel will He gather in."[174] The fact that these two

---

174 *Tehillim* 147:2.

themes are juxtaposed is not lost on the commentaries: when you see the city of Yerushalayim building up with construction and inhabitants, then He will gather all the dispersed to Yerushalayim from the ends of the earth.[175]

The prophet Yeshayah speaks of the ruins of Yerushalayim that will be rebuilt: "As for your ruins and desolations, and your devastated land, you will now become crowded with inhabitants, and

> One of the precursors to the arrival of the Mashiach: the rebuilding and population burst inside Yerushalayim.

those who devour you will become distanced."[176] Rashi comments on this phenomenon by explaining that Yerushalayim before the advent of the Messianic era is going to be so full of inhabitants that there will not be enough room to build houses for everybody.

If you travel to Yerushalayim today, you can't miss the constant building of new apartment buildings all over the city. I travel with students to Israel a few times a year and I'm still astonished by the incredible speed at which beautiful buildings are erected when just a little while before, all that could be seen in those areas were empty lots!

The prophet concludes with a feeling we have all felt when seeing the Land of Israel grow in all its splendor: "And you will say in your heart, 'Who has begotten me these…where are these from?'" Yeshayah is asking a rhetorical question: when you see Yerushalayim, you will be overcome with great joy and you'll marvel at how the once bereaved city of Yerushalayim has transformed and is now bustling with so many inhabitants, and you'll ask, how is all this change and growth even possible?

ISRAEL AND YERUSHALAYIM WILL EXPAND

With the return of the Jews to Israel and Yerushalayim, more room will be needed to house all the new inhabitants. Even with all this overcrowding in preparation for the Mashiach's arrival, there will miraculously be enough room for everyone to reside comfortably somewhere in the

---

175 *Metzudos David, Tehillim* ibid.
176 *Yeshayah* 49:19.

Land of Israel. The Torah tells us that the Land of Israel was promised to Avraham when G-d said to him, "To your descendants have I given this Land, from the river of Egypt the great river, the Euphrates River."[177] The Torah then lists the ten nations that would exist in the Land that would need to be driven out in the future. Rashi comments, "Ten nations are mentioned here, but He only gave the Jewish people the land of seven nations. The final three, Edom, Moav, and Ammon — who are the Kenite, Kenizzite, and Kadmonite of our verse — are destined to be an inheritance for Israel in the future." This means that those lands were not conquered by Yehoshua but will be part of Israel when the Mashiach takes his leadership position over the Jewish people.

The prophet Zechariah spoke of seeing a vision of a man holding a measuring line. When the prophet asked him where he was going, he said, "To measure Yerushalayim, to see how wide its breadth and how long its length."[178] According to the commentators, this was a vision foretelling events that will take place during the days of the Mashiach. Why did he need to measure it? Because he was comparing the size of the Yerushalayim of Zechariah's day and that of the great increase the city will have when the Mashiach actually does arrive. This is because when the Mashiach arrives (and perhaps in preparation for his imminent arrival), Yerushalayim will see a great increase in size, as one would expect of the greatest city in the world, which will be the focus of every nation's attention before and after Mashiach comes.[179]

This growth is what Zechariah meant when he said, "Yerushalayim will be settled beyond its walls, because of the multitude of people and livestock within it. And I will be for it a wall of fire all around and for glory will I be in its midst."[180] The Talmud interprets this to mean that the "man" (who was actually an angel of G-d) was told to stop measuring the walls of the city, because since the city of Yerushalayim will

---

177   *Bereishis* 15:18–19.

178   *Zechariah* 2:1.

179   Radak, *Zechariah* 2:7.

180   Ibid. v. 8–9.

increase so much, it will not be limited to any set area.[181] Zechariah was being told that Yerushalayim will be settled beyond its walls so that all who wish to come and dwell within it will do so and thereby increase its population day by day.

YECHEZKEL'S VISION OF THE THIRD AND FINAL TEMPLE

The prophet Yechezkel was given a rare and detailed vision of the Third and final Temple in Yerushalayim. This is crucial because, as we've already discussed, one of the most important ways that the Mashiach can prove that he is the promised redeemer is by rebuilding the Third Temple on the Temple Mount in Yerushalayim.

When G-d asked Yechezkel the Prophet to give his prophecy to the people, he became quite concerned. He reasoned that the Jews had been exiled from the Land and the Temple had been destroyed. According to the Midrash, Yechezkel asked G-d, "We are now in exile in the land of our enemies, and you tell me to go and tell Israel the design of the Third Temple. Wouldn't it be better to leave them be and wait until they reenter the Land before I tell them?"

G-d responded by saying, "Is it right that because My children are in exile the building of My Temple should be ignored?" So G-d told Yechezkel that "by studying and discussing the Third Temple and its structure, it is considered equal in merit to actually building it." He then commanded Yechezkel to "go tell them to study the Temple structure and as a reward I will consider their study as though they were actually building the Temple."

Yechezkel was taken in a prophetic vision to see the destroyed First Temple. As it says in *Yechezkel*, "In a Divine vision He brought me to the Land; He set me down on a very high mountain, near which there was something like the structure of a city to the south."[182] This "very high mountain" is a reference to the Temple Mount in Yerushalayim, which although high now, will be considerably higher in Messianic times.[183]

---

181   *Bava Basra* 75b with Rashbam's commentary.
182   *Yechezkel* 40:2.
183   Rashi, ibid.

THE THIRD TEMPLE:
NOT JUST ARCHITECTURAL CHALLENGES

The *Akeidas Yitzchak* explains that the building of the Third Temple will consist of more than just sound building plans and architecture.[184] In a time that only G-d decides, an enduring structure will be built, such as that envisaged in the concluding chapters of *Sefer Yechezkel*. That, however, will only be once the Jewish people will have become so refined in character through having been persecuted in exile that success can be ensured and the Divine Presence would not again be forced to withdraw.

The entire *Sefer Yechezkel* can be viewed as concentrating on this subject, seeing that it commences with a vision of *maaseh merkavah*, i.e., G-d's residence in the heavens, and concludes with visions of G-d's residence on earth. The intervening chapters only provide the rationale why a permanent residence for G-d on earth had not yet been possible — due to the errant ways of G-d's Chosen People. Only after the fulfillment of "and I shall sprinkle on you cleansing waters...and give you a new heart,"[185] have the conditions been met that must precede the establishment of a permanent home for G-d on this earth.

Building the Third Temple won't just entail architectural abilities but also prophetic ones. A number of questions about the precise location of the Temple and the exact placement of many of the Temple's items can only be ascertained through prophetic vision. For example, the Altar cannot be placed anywhere within the Temple precinct except for the exact location where it was in Shlomo HaMelech's Temple. When the Second Temple was built after the Babylonian exile, the place of the Altar had to be revealed prophetically to Ezra. The same will be true in the Messianic era. Every item in the new Temple will have to be placed in the correct location — something only a prophet of G-d can reveal to us.

The Mashiach will have the prophetic power to identify the precise location for every item in the Temple. He and only he will have that

---

184   *Akeidas Yitzchak* 50:1.
185   *Yechezkel* 36:25–26.

ability and he will use his senses to locate and establish every part of the Temple in Yerushalayim. No one but a great prophet can have the power and ability to do this.

A GREAT PROPHET OF G-D FOR ALL MANKIND

The Rambam gives us a short biographical sketch of what the Mashiach will actually be like: "The Mashiach will be a king descended from David HaMelech, he will be even wiser than Shlomo HaMelech (who was known as the wisest of all men). His level of prophecy will approach that of Moshe Rabbeinu."[186] The Mashiach cannot be greater than Moshe Rabbeinu, as another principle of our faith, according to the Rambam, is that no prophet will ever exceed or even parallel the level of the prophecy of Moshe Rabbeinu, the greatest prophet in world history. The prophecy of Moshe Rabbeinu is the Torah, also known as the "Five Books of Moses" for that very reason, and is where the 613 mitzvos in the Torah are recorded. No prophet, not even the Mashiach, will be able to retract any part of the Torah himself.

His impact on the world will be unparalleled in world history. People mistakenly believe that the arrival of the Mashiach will affect only the Jewish people; however the entire world will know of the Mashiach and will attempt to meet this great individual, as the prophet Yeshayah predicts: "At the End of Days the mountain of G-d's House (the Temple in Yerushalayim) will be firmly established as the head of the mountains, and shall be set high above the hills, and all the nations will stream to it. Many people will go and say, 'Come, let us go up to the mountain of G-d...and He will teach us His ways and we will walk in His path.'"[187]

Even though this event or series of events will be taking place in the rebuilt Third Temple in Yerushalayim, since all the nations of the world will be aware of the arrival of the Mashiach, different people will stream into Yerushalayim to hear from the Mashiach himself and to rejoice in

---

186   Rambam, *Mishneh Torah, Teshuvah* 9:2.
187   *Yeshayah* 2:2–3.

his words. As all humans are made in the image of G-d, they will now turn their attention to the one true G-d of Israel.

Rashi says that the expression for "streaming," *naharu*, connotes that all the nations will gather together like a stream to the Temple, like rivers coming together and swiftly flowing to the sea. The Vilna Gaon says that this stream of people may also represent the method they will use to get there, i.e., over streams, rivers, oceans, and seas. The word *nahar*, literally river, refers not only to a flow of water but also to a stream of light. This, says Rabbi Samson Raphael Hirsch, means that the spiritual light that will emanate from Yerushalayim in those days will attract everybody's attention — man and woman, young and old, Jew and non-Jew — and each will feel the incredible pull of this spiritual light.[188]

THE RETURN OF PROPHECY TO ISRAEL AND TO ALL THE JEWISH PEOPLE

The Mashiach will be a prophet, second only in his prophetic ability to Moshe Rabbeinu.[189] However, before he arrives, he will be announced by Eliyahu, who himself will be a prophet. This, say the prophets, is the proof that before the Mashiach actually arrives, prophecy will return to the Jewish people. As the final prophet Malachi says in his final prophecy, "Behold I send you Eliyahu HaNavi before the coming of the great and awesome day of Hashem."[190] This is necessary because the Mashiach will be a king — and a king can only be anointed by a prophet.

The restoration of prophecy is a very important prelude to the arrival of the Mashiach. So when we talk of *Bi'as HaMashiach*, the coming of the Mashiach, this refers to the moment when the Mashiach receives this spirit of prophecy and realizes his mission.[191]

---

188   Rabbi Samson Raphael Hirsch, *Tehillim* 34:6.

189   *Sefer Ha'Ikarim, Maamar Shlishi*, chap. 20 understands the Rambam differently. The idea that "no prophet shall be like Moshe Rabbeinu" only refers to the prophets that have lived in the past. However, the Rambam did not mean to include a prophet in the future who may well be on the same level as Moshe Rabbeinu, which would include the Mashiach and his prophetic ability.

190   *Malachi* 3:23.

191   *Arba Meos Shekel Kessef* (Krakow 5646), pg. 68c.

The prophet Yoel goes as far as to say that prophecy will not just be given to the leaders or great men and women among our people, but will become a widespread phenomenon. Let's look at the incredible words of the prophet Yoel to see the implications of this widespread prophetic ability that will be bestowed onto the masses: "And it will happen after this, that I will pour out My spirit upon all flesh, and your sons and daughters will prophesy; your elders will dream prophetic dreams, and your young men will see visions."[192] This is a reference to the entire Jewish people being endowed with prophetic ability — men, women, and even children. Others contend that in fact all mankind will achieve this clear recognition of G-d, but only the Jews will achieve the prophetic ability of which the prophet speaks.

The Chafetz Chaim reminds us that the entire Jewish people were all prophets once before in Jewish history.[193] When we all stood at Mount Sinai, every man, woman, and child was given the power of prophecy in order to receive the Torah directly from G-d. This happened when G-d gave us the first two of the Ten Commandments. So intense was this experience that the people were not able to hear more than the first two and begged Moshe Rabbeinu to act as the prophet to receive the rest of the Torah on their behalf.

When the Mashiach comes, we will once again be able to learn Torah directly from G-d and become prophets in our own right. In order to be worthy of this future prophecy, continues the Chafetz Chaim, we must accept the Torah, learn the Torah before his arrival, and accept the mitzvos, which means we should perform them to the best of our ability. The more we invest our lives with Torah and mitzvos, the more we will be able to benefit from the incredible revelation when the Mashiach does finally appear.

A CHILD'S VERSUS AN ADULT'S PROPHETIC POWERS

Why does the prophet Yoel describe the visions of children as "prophecy" and the visions of elders as merely "dreams"? Usually the power

---

192   *Yoel* 3:1.
193   Chafetz Chaim, *Shem Olam* 12.

of prophecy was attained only by great men and women who worked very hard on developing their prophetic powers. Even though prophecy is a gift bestowed upon the person by G-d, just as intellect can grow through hard work and mental toil, so too, says the Rambam, can a person grow in their prophetic powers through Torah study, spiritual pursuits, and prayers. Because of this, children and the masses were not able to achieve any form of prophetic powers, as the ability to reach the heights of spiritual visions was not available to them, due to their young age or lack of other responsibilities.

However, in the times of the Mashiach, G-d's spirit, says Yoel, will pervade all people, no matter their age or life status. According to the Malbim, since young children will be born into an era where G-d's presence is so palpable, they will attain the highest level of prophecy — *nevu'ah*. The elders, on the other hand, since they will have matured in a non-prophetic time, much prior to the Redemption, their level of prophecy will not reach the level of the young children and will remain at the level of *chalomos*, dreams. In between dreams and full prophecy is a level called *chezyonos*, visions. This level will be attained by youths who will be born before the Redemption but will reach adulthood during the Messianic era.

THE JEWISH RETURN TO ISRAEL AND PROPHECY RETURNING — WHAT'S THE CONNECTION?

As we have already seen, the restoration of prophecy is a very important part of the unfolding of the Messianic drama. However, a few conditions need to be met before prophecy can be fully reintroduced to the Jewish people.

Firstly, prophecy can only take place in the Land of Israel and not in any other country. History has shown us that there are exceptions to this rule. For example, Yonah the Prophet was commanded to leave Israel and go northeast to the city of Nineveh to prophesy. His job was to warn the people of the impending doom their city faced if they didn't repent to G-d for their evil ways. Nineveh was outside of Israel and Yonah was a prophet. Still, it was necessary for Yonah to give his prophecy to this non-Jewish city even though it was outside of Israel. Even so, the prophecy he was to give the people of Nineveh was received by Yonah while he was still in the Land of Israel, as the Land itself is highly conducive to receiving prophecy from G-d.

Another condition necessary for the return of prophecy is that the majority of the Jewish people must be residing in the Land of Israel in order for the prophet to receive his or her prophecy. This is based upon the verse in the Torah, "G-d your Lord will raise up a prophet in your midst."[194] Israel is only considered "in your midst" when the majority of the Jewish people are residing in it. This means that of all the Jewish people in the entire world — ideally all or at least fifty percent of them — need to be living in the Land of Israel.

By having most of the Jews in the world living in Israel, the spiritual energy conducive to prophecy is concentrated enough to permit the power of prophecy to exist in Israel. This means that the prophet didn't just receive prophecy whenever he willed it. Rather, prophecy came to him when he was able to channel the power of the many Jews residing in the holy Land of Israel. The prophet then received prophecy because of the people he was surrounded by in Israel, not despite of them.

So unless we assume this rule is to be broken, and there's no reason to think as such, more than half of the Jewish people will have to live in the Land of Israel before the Messianic era commences.

WHERE ARE MOST OF THE JEWS TODAY?

As of September 2016, the State of Israel had a population of 8.585 million people, 172,000 more than the same time one year previous to that. With 6.4 million residents, Jews make up close to three-quarters of the population, while Israel's almost 1.8 million Arabs make up one-fifth of the population. Those of other backgrounds, including non-Arab Christians and those not categorized as members of a religious group, make up less than five percent of the population, at 380,000 people.[195]

---

194   *Devarim* 18:15.
195   http://www.timesofisrael.com/on-rosh-hashanah-eve-israels-population-hits-8-58-million/.

At the time of its founding in 1948, Israel had a little over 800,000 people (including Jews and non-Jews). That was six percent of the Jews in the world.

According to the Diaspora Affairs Ministry's statistics, there are currently 14.4 million Jews in the world, with 6.3 million in Israel and the rest spread out over the globe.[196] We are therefore close to the fifty-percent tipping point, which is the threshold to allow prophecy to recommence and the Mashiach to announce his arrival.

---

196 http://www.israelnationalnews.com/News/News.aspx/221859.

Chapter Twelve

HOW TO SHORTEN THE EXILE

WITH ALL THE talk of great miracles and incredible events happening in Israel before and after the Mashiach's arrival, one miracle stands out among them all: Jewish unity. The prophet Yechezkel says: "And I will make them into one nation in the Land upon the mountains of Israel, and one king shall be to them all as a king."[197] The Mashiach will have a monumental task of uniting the Jewish people. This unification is not merely a geographical unity, but a unity of peace that will need to spread over Jewish communities wherever they are.

The power of unity among the Jewish people isn't just a nice idea; it's a crucial element in the advent of the Messianic era and the revelation of the Mashiach himself. The rebuilding of the Temple in Yerushalayim and the key to our redemption, says the Sfas Emes, is by loving our fellow Jews: "Since the Temple was destroyed by baseless hatred, therefore, it will surely be rebuilt by loving our fellow Jews."[198] This helps us understand the Talmud that states: "Every generation that does not build the Temple, it is as though they destroyed it."[199] This, says the Chasam Sofer, is hinted at in the *Ha Lachma Anya* section of the Pesach Haggadah. There, we are shown that we can expedite our redemption

---

197   *Yechezkel* 37:22.
198   Sfas Emes, *Rosh Hashanah*, 5641.
199   Talmud Yerushalmi, *Yoma* 1:1.

through good deeds, specifically those deeds that involve mitzvos that are *bein adam lechaveiro*, mitzvos between us and each other.

Charity hastening the Redemption is referred to by the prophet Yeshayah and mentioned in the Talmud: "It is taught in a Baraisa that Rabbi Yehudah says: Great is charity in that it hastens the Redemption, as it is stated: 'So said Hashem, uphold justice and do charity, for My salvation is near to come, and My righteousness to be revealed.'"[200] The Maharsha comments that acts of charity performed by the Jewish people will bring the Final Redemption, and at that time there will be a revelation of G-d's acts of charity, which are now concealed.

The *Ben Yehoyada* questions why the verse mentions "justice," inasmuch as Rabbi Yehudah said only "charity" brings the redemption closer. He explains that charity has this effect only when the money donated is justly obtained by the giver. Money acquired by dishonest means is not acceptable to G-d when offered as charity. Therefore "charity" alone does have the power to bring the redemption closer, and so Yeshayah mentions "justice" as well in order to define which type of charity is meant.

JEWISH UNITY — THE KEY TO BRINGING THE EXILE TO A SPEEDY END

The Chasam Sofer explains that we are capable of ending this exile through acts of kindness. That is why at the beginning of the Passover Seder we invite guests into our homes saying, "Whoever is hungry come and join the Seder," and then we conclude the *Ha Lachma Anya* section itself by saying, "This year here — next year in the Land of Israel!" It's in the merit of taking care of our fellow Jews that we can redeem ourselves from exile. Thus the Pesach Seder culminates with the hope and prayer of the final and greatest redemption, i.e., the rebuilding of the Temple, with the statement, "Next year in Yerushalayim." It all starts, however, with taking care of guests.

Let's first see how Yerushalayim was divided, and then maybe we can work out how to unify it again.

---

200   *Yeshayah* 56:1; *Bava Basra* 10a.

KAMTZA AND BAR KAMTZA

The Talmud tells the famous story of two people, Kamtza and Bar Kamtza. It was their actions, says the Talmud, which led to the destruction of the Second Temple in Yerushalayim.[201] According to some, Kamtza and Bar Kamtza were father and son. A certain wealthy man was throwing a lavish party and invited all the dignitaries to this special event. He had a friend named Kamtza, however, Kamtza's son, Bar Kamtza, was his enemy. He told his servant, "Go and invite Kamtza to the party." However, the servant misheard and went and invited the wrong guest, Bar Kamtza, his enemy, instead.

The party began and when the host saw Bar Kamtza was there, he approached him and said in front of all the guests, "You are my enemy; what are you doing here? I didn't invite you! Get out!" To avoid the incredible shame he must have felt at this slight to his honor, Bar Kamtza responded, "Since I am already here, let me stay, and I will pay you for whatever I eat and drink." The host refused, saying, "No, leave my party now!" Bar Kamtza, not wishing to make a scene, pleaded with the man and said, "I'm here now, please let me stay and I'll pay for half the entire party." The host once again refused his offer. "Please, I'll pay for the entire feast! Just let me stay and don't embarrass me!" Still the host refused and Bar Kamtza was forced to stand up in front of all the dignitaries in Yerushalayim and leave the event, his head down in obvious shame.

This event, relates the Talmud, was the catalyst for the eventual destruction of the Temple in Yerushalayim. After being publicly shamed, without even one of the rabbis present saying anything to the host in his defense, Bar Kamtza became furious. This one incident was the seed for Bar Kamtza becoming an enemy of his own people. He took revenge by acting as a traitor against the Jews by reporting falsehoods to the Romans, who were controlling Israel at the time.

Had the host of this party shown greater consideration to Bar Kamtza and found the ability to forgive him, or at the least not embarrass him

---

201   *Gittin* 55a–56b.

publicly, the Temple in Yerushalayim would still be standing and the Jewish people wouldn't have been exiled from our land, Israel.

Why would this incident represent the reason for the Temple's destruction and the exile of the Jewish people from the Land for over two thousand years? In order to answer this question, we need to understand the power of peace in our communities and the destructive power of *lashon hara*, destructive gossip, in keeping us in exile.

KEEPING PEACE IN OUR COMMUNITIES

Rav Eliezer in the Talmud was asked by his students, "What should a person do to be saved from the suffering of *chevlei Mashiach*, the suffering that will accompany the coming of the Mashiach?" He answered, "A person should occupy himself with Torah study and *gemilus chasadim*, act of loving-kindness one to another."[202]

The amazing impact acts of kindness can have in the world is a key theme in much of the writings of the Chafetz Chaim. As he writes in *Shemiras HaLashon*, the Mashiach will come when we maintain peace in our communities by eradicating both baseless hatred and derogatory speech about other people:

> *It is written in the name of the holy Zohar that even one congregation that maintains peace properly can merit bringing the Mashiach. Therefore, the coming of the Mashiach is dependent upon us. And it is known that preserving peace can only be accomplished if we are careful in avoiding both baseless hatred and speaking derogatorily of one another. Each individual who endeavors to rectify these shortcomings will have a share in rebuilding the future Temple; without this, the Temple could remain destroyed forever, G-d forbid.*[203]

---

202 *Sanhedrin* 98b.
203 Chafetz Chaim, *Sefer Chafetz Chaim* 2:7.

According to the Chafetz Chaim, therefore, the key element in redemption is peace between ourselves. The way peace is broken and strife usually begins is through negative and destructive speech, what we call *lashon hara*. All division and all arguments that come between people always involve negative and destructive speech. So bad is this sin, says the Chafetz Chaim, that it is what has kept the Mashiach from coming over the past two thousand years and what has prevented the building of the Third and final Temple in Yerushalayim.

> The key element in redemption is peace between ourselves.

Even Moshe Rabbeinu himself was aware of how negative speech prevented redemption. The Torah tells us about Moshe Rabbeinu as a young man living as a prince in Egypt. On one occasion, he saw an Egyptian taskmaster beating an innocent Jewish man to the point of death. This injustice moved Moshe Rabbeinu to action and he struck the Egyptian, killing him on the spot and saving the Jew's life. A short time later, Moshe Rabbeinu encountered two Jewish men fighting and arguing with each other.

Moshe Rabbeinu approached the men and attempted to bring peace between them, as it says, "And he went out the second day, and, behold, two men of the Hebrews were fighting together; and he said to him that did the wrong, 'Why are you striking your fellow?'

"The man responded, 'Who made you a ruler and a judge over us? Do you want to kill me, like you killed the Egyptian?' Moshe Rabbeinu responded to this comment of the man by saying, 'Surely the matter is known.'"[204]

The Torah does not inform us what "matter" Moshe Rabbeinu is concerned about being known. The commentators interpret his comment in different ways. By the man making this statement, Moshe Rabbeinu became aware of what had kept the Jewish people in exile all these years: *lashon hara*, destructive speech. The fact that these men were aware that Moshe Rabbeinu had killed the Egyptian and buried him in the sand

---

204 *Shemos* 2:13–14.

means that people had been speaking *lashon hara* about him and that was "the matter now known" — that gossip had kept the Jews in exile all this time. If they wanted to go free, the Jewish people would have to work on improving their speech to and about each other.

TAKING REVENGE AND BEARING GRUDGES

Two areas of interpersonal mitzvos that people sometimes overlook, are *lo sikom*, not taking revenge, and *lo sitor*, not bearing a grudge.

Not taking revenge or bearing a grudge seem to play a central role in the story of Kamtza and Bar Kamtza and are therefore areas we need to work on to be worthy of Mashiach. The Chafetz Chaim in his *Concise List of Mitzvos* (mitzvos we are able to perform today) lists these two negative commandments as their own separate prohibitions. He defines revenge as repaying a person who has harmed you in the same way that he treated you. For example, if you asked to borrow an item from someone, and he refused, and then he wishes to borrow one of your items, which you perhaps would have normally lent him but don't in order to exact revenge, you have transgressed a Torah prohibition.

Bearing a grudge is connected to taking revenge, but potentially much worse. If, in the above example, after not lending you an item, your friend asks you for something, and while you do lend them, you keep hatred in your heart by saying or maybe even thinking, "I'm not like you; I'm kind and caring, and I lend things," you have transgressed the sin of bearing a grudge. The challenge with bearing a grudge is that unlike revenge, the hate is less evident and may remain only in your heart. This is exactly what the Torah wants us to avoid.

The Chafetz Chaim refers to these two character defects as *ra'os me'od*, extremely bad. He then gives a short piece of advice in how to overcome them: "All matters and concerns of this world are *hevel*, vapid nonsense and triviality, and it is not worth taking revenge over them." His use of the word *hevel* is certainly deliberate and reminds us of the words of Shlomo HaMelech at the start of *Koheles* when he calls all of existence *hevel havalim*, vanity of vanities. The word *hevel* also means "steam." Though steam looks and feels real, and can even burn you, it's just air that will soon dissipate.

Had the players in the Kamtza and Bar Kamtza story been aware of all these ideas and given up on their desire for revenge — bearing a grudge, holding anger in their hearts, and being careful with their words — the Beis Hamikdash would still be standing today. By being attentive of how we treat others, we may merit the Third and final Beis Hamikdash being built for us!

Let's now examine another area of Jewish life that the Sages tell us can also bring the present exile to an end: Shabbos.

Chapter Thirteen

SHABBOS — THE GREAT REDEEMER

OF ALL THE mitzvos given to the Jewish people, Shabbos is considered one of the most valuable and important mitzvos. Shabbos has within it all there is to know about being Jewish. It's Shabbos — not Pesach, Shavuos, Succos, or even Yom Kippur — that is mentioned in the Ten Commandments. Shabbos is considered greater and more holy than any other day in the Jewish calendar. Very importantly, it will be in the merit of the Shabbos that the Mashiach will come and redeem the world. Let's try to understand why.

The first time the word *berachah*, blessing, is mentioned in the Torah is in relation to G-d creating fish: "G-d blessed them, saying, 'Be fruitful and multiply, and fill the waters in the seas.'"[205] Why would fish need to be blessed? Fish are in need of special blessings due to the fact that so many are hunted down and eaten. The power of G-d's blessing allows the fish to exist in vast numbers even after being preyed upon by mankind and other fish. So the Hebrew word for "blessing" also means "plentiful."

The second time the word "blessing" appears is in relation to Shabbos: "G-d blessed the seventh day and sanctified it."[206] How can a day be blessed? The answer is that the power of blessing can exist on a day as

---

205 *Bereishis* 1:22.
206 Ibid. 2:3.

well. This means that the day itself, i.e., the observance of the mitzvos of Shabbos, brings the power of blessing to a person who performs them. Just like fish were blessed with plenty, so too Shabbos has the ability to bring plenty of blessings to those who keep it.

On Friday night, in the prayerful song *Lechah Dodi*, we sing about the blessing ability of Shabbos. The author of that song refers to Shabbos as the *mekor haberachah*, the source of all blessing. By this he means that all blessings that exist in this world find their source in Shabbos itself.

> All blessings that exist in this world find their source in Shabbos.

We can use an analogy to understand this better.

Imagine you are walking in a desert and then suddenly enter a garden with plenty of trees, flowers, fruits, and vegetables. As you walk around the garden, you wonder how such lush vegetation could come into a dry region such as this. As you walk deeper into this glorious garden, you see a pool of fresh water. This pool is overflowing with water and has even created channels that branch out into different parts of the garden. You soon realize that this pool is the entire reason that the garden was able to develop into the beautiful garden you see before you.

The days of the week are like a garden. Each day has amazing potential to bring us unlimited joy and success. The pool in the center of the week is Shabbos. The reason we are successful on Tuesday afternoon or Thursday morning is because of the blessing power of Shabbos. The blessing flows from that day into the other days of the week, just like the water from the pool flows into the rest of the garden. Shabbos brings with it many merits, and each one enhances our lives incredibly.

SHABBOS — THE GREAT GIFT

Shabbos is the only mitzvah that G-d Himself refers to as a *matanah tovah*, a great gift. The Talmud says in *Shabbos*, "G-d said to Moshe, 'I have a special gift in my treasure house, it's called Shabbos, [and] I wish to give it to the Jewish people. Go and notify them.'"[207]

---

207 *Shabbos* 10b.

The commentators have different opinions as to what the exact nature of the gift of Shabbos actually is. One opinion is that the gift is the great reward we receive for keeping Shabbos. Another opinion, however, says that the great gift that comes from observing Shabbos is two-fold: it protects the Jewish people from being attacked and harmed by other nations, and it acts as a way to give the Jewish people speedy redemption from their exile. Let's look a little deeper at both of these explanations.

SHABBOS — THE JEWISH DEFENSE FORCE

When the Jewish people were in the Sinai Desert after leaving Egypt, they were given the mitzvah of keeping Shabbos. However, soon after receiving it, some among the nation broke the laws of Shabbos. Right after the Torah describes the episode of the profaned Shabbos, it relates what on the surface seems like an unrelated episode: the nation of Amalek coming to attack the Jewish people. These two events, the breaking of the second-ever Shabbos and the attack of Amalek, says Rabbi Yonasan Eibshitz, are very much related.[208] Shabbos acts as a protective barrier between the Jewish people and the other nations. Once the Jewish people broke Shabbos, that protection was partly removed, and the nation of Amalek was able to grab the opportunity and break through to attack us.

Shabbos is the source of blessing, it's a great gift, and it protects our people from outside physical and spiritual harm. When putting these ideas together, a pattern of the redemptive quality of Shabbos emerges — that Shabbos saves us. This idea was historically recognized not only by the Jews, but even by enemies of the Jews. The Talmud tells us that Vashti would humiliate the Jewish women by making them do work on Shabbos.[209] What did Vashti hope to achieve by tormenting her Jewish subjects in this way?

Rabbi Yonasan Eibshitz says that this testifies to the incredible power of Shabbos — that even an evil person like Vashti knew the importance

---

208   Rabbi Yonasan Eibshitz, *Yaaros Devash* 8b, *Derash* 3.
209   *Megillah* 12b.

of that special day, and by making the Jewish women break Shabbos, she could keep them in exile and prevent their redemption.[210] Her plan did not work, as these women were forced to break Shabbos and therefore were not held liable for their actions. Notably, G-d acted *middah keneged middah*, measure for measure against Vashti, and that's why the Megillah itself tells us she met her demise "on the seventh day," which was Shabbos.

JUST ONE SHABBOS AND WE'LL ALL BE FREE!

The Talmud quotes Rabbi Shimon Bar Yochai who said, "If the Jewish people keep two Shabboses, they would be immediately redeemed."[211] According to the *Midrash Rabbah*, the power of Shabbos is such that even one Shabbos would suffice to redeem the Jewish people.[212]

What is it about Shabbos that gives it this ability of shortening the exile? The Midrash explains that since Shabbos is equal to all the mitzvos in the Torah, by keeping Shabbos we are in effect keeping all the mitzvos, even those that we are incapable of keeping today. The merit of all Jews keeping Shabbos is enough to bring the Redemption and end our current state of exile.

Thus the observance of Shabbos, says the *Shnei Luchos HaBris*, has a two-fold significance. It is a prototype of the rest that follows the completion of the Creation as well as a prototype of the freedom that followed the end of slavery. "While striving to restore its unity with the Creator, Israel also restores the original grandeur and purity of the Creation. While struggling to restore its union with its Deliverer, Israel also regains its own freedom and security on earth."[213] So as we celebrate Shabbos we are reconnecting to the Creation of the world and the creation of the Jewish people after the Exodus from Egypt. By doing this we are meriting the Final Redemption, the Mashiach's arrival.

---

210   *Yaaros Devash* 2:2.
211   *Shabbos* 118b.
212   *Shemos* 25:12.
213   *VeZos HaBerachah, Derech Chaim Tochachos Mussar*, 167.

A TASTE OF THE NEXT WORLD

What is the Jewish view of heaven? How do you explain a spiritual environment that is not physical in any way? The answer the rabbis give to describe the future world is quite unusual in that it's called, "the world that is all Shabbos." What does that even mean? How could a place or time be "all Shabbos"? The answer is in understanding what the nature of Shabbos really is: Shabbos is a microcosm of the Next World.

The Talmud goes on to say that if you prepare on Erev Shabbos, you will have what to eat on Shabbos. Isn't that obvious? You cannot prepare and cook food on Shabbos, so obviously that which you cook before Shabbos will be all you can eat on Shabbos. However, once we look a little deeper, we see that the Shabbos being referred to over here is not the Shabbos as we know it, but *Olam Haba*, the future world that is compared to Shabbos. So this world is Erev Shabbos, and the Next World is Shabbos itself.

If we prepare ourselves in the Present World, it's as though we are "cooking" and preparing ourselves for the Next World where we receive reward for our actions. If we don't use this world and its opportunities for the good, then we won't be able to enjoy the fruits of our labor in the Next World; we won't have what to "eat" in the Next World.

Shabbos is really the gateway into the Next World, the world of Mashiach and beyond. It's for this reason that the rabbis point out the power of Shabbos as the ability to not only allow you to access the Next World but to even shorten the length of the exile totally and to bring the Redemption even quicker than before. How do we activate that speedy redemption? By keeping Shabbos.

We have two aspects to keeping Shabbos. One is to perform all the positive mitzvos of Shabbos, such as lighting candles on Friday night, eating three meals over the course of the Shabbos, enjoying and celebrating this special and holy day, and concluding with the *Havdalah* ceremony. The second is refraining from the creative acts, called *melachos*, which are forbidden to perform. These two facets of keeping Shabbos, more than any other mitzvah (except for Torah study itself), can bring the exile to a successful and much-awaited end!

The Talmud is asking us all to improve our observance by reviewing the halachos of Shabbos and spending our precious time on Shabbos more wisely. What are we discussing at the Shabbos table? How are we acting towards others on this special and holy day? We all can make more out of the Shabbos, which Hashem Himself called an *oneg*, delight.

Chapter Fourteen

STUDY TORAH AND SET YOURSELF FREE

THE HOLIEST OBJECT we have as Jews is the Torah. We keep the Torah in the front of the synagogue on the eastern wall towards the direction of Israel. Not only that, but unlike a book that is just kept on a shelf, the Torah is stored in an *aron*, ark, and then a curtain is added on the outside to notify us of the holy contents of this ark.

The greatest mitzvah the Jewish people have is to study G-d's Torah. The *Zohar* tells us that when G-d created the universe, He, so to speak, looked into the Torah and created the world based on what is written in it.[214] So when we study Torah we are connecting to G-d Himself and His purpose for Creation. When we perform the mitzvos enumerated in the Torah, we as Jews are fulfilling our mission in this world.

The Rambam makes a point of explaining that if the Torah was given to all the Jewish people, and can improve the lot of the entire world, it is therefore a mitzvah for all Jews to study and not just for some academically-inclined individuals. As the Rambam says, "Every Jewish man is obligated in the study of Torah, whether he is poor or rich, whether he is in good health or is suffering, young or very old and weak; even if he is so poor that he is living on charity and begging at doorways; even one who must support a wife and

---

214 *Zohar, Terumah* 161a.

children is obligated to set aside time, every day and every night, for the study of Torah."[215]

So no matter what your station in life is, studying Torah must be part of it. Some Sages throughout Jewish history were from very wealthy homes and others were extremely poor. Some had health issues that disrupted their lives and others had to work to support large families. Irrespective of where one is in life, one still has a mitzvah to set aside some time each day to study Torah. In the words of the Rambam, "Among the great Sages of Israel were woodchoppers and water-bearers, and some who were blind. Nevertheless, they engaged in the study of Torah day and night, and they were part of the chain of transmission of the Torah, person to person, back to Moshe Rabbeinu."

Torah is the backbone of the Jewish people. Without it, the Jewish people would not be here and maybe the entire world wouldn't be here either.

TORAH HAS INFLUENCED THE NON-JEWISH WORLD

Torah hasn't just influenced the Jewish people and made us who we are as a people, it has also had a major impact on the world as a whole. Paul Johnson in *A History of the Jews* makes the case that the world without Jewish scholarship and Torah learning would have been a radically different place. As he explains: "Humanity might have eventually stumbled upon all the Jewish insights. But we cannot be sure. All the great conceptual discoveries of the human intellect seem obvious and inescapable once they had been revealed, but it requires a special genius to formulate them for the first time. The Jews had this gift."[216]

According to Johnson, some of the ways the Torah has influenced humanity is:

- Equality before the law, both Divine and human
- The sanctity of life and the dignity of a human person

---

215 Rambam, *Mishneh Torah, Talmud Torah* 1:8.
216 Paul Johnson, *A History of the Jews* (Harper Collins, 1987), pg. 585.

- The individual conscience, and so a personal redemption
- Collective conscience, and so of social responsibility
- Peace as an abstract ideal
- Love as the foundation of justice

But Torah has a bigger role for every individual and for humanity as a whole: it prepares us for *Olam Haba*. Not only that, studying Torah also reduces the amount of time we spend in exile and brings the end of the exile closer. Let's see how this actually works.

TORAH — YOUR PASSPORT TO OLAM HABA

The Mishnah in *Pirkei Avos* tells us that, "If a person acquires a good name, he does so for himself. But if he acquires Torah, he acquires life in the World to Come."[217]

If learning Torah is considered so great, then teaching Torah to many students is facilitating other people's learning and in turn is an even greater mitzvah, as one spreads G-d's teachings to the world. Teaching Torah in this world, says the Talmud, will even permit one to teach Torah in the World to Come.[218]

Not only does Torah study improve one's experience of the Next World, it also shortens the amount of time we are in exile without the Mashiach. It brings the Next World even closer.

What's the connection between Torah study, the shortening of the exile, and a person's position in the Next World (after the Messianic Revelation)?

The practical answer is that by studying Torah, we are learning what the 613 mitzvos are and how to perform them. By performing mitzvos, we are fulfilling our mission for mankind and thereby shortening the necessity for staying in exile in the first place.

How does studying Torah shorten the length of the exile and bring us redemption? The answer is quite incredible: Torah is the thought

---

217   *Pirkei Avos* 2:7.
218   *Sanhedrin* 92a.

process of G-d, so to speak, meaning it's His will for this world. When we study Torah, we are actually connecting our mind to the Creator of the entire world. G-d created the world, but is not limited to only existing in this world. So when we study Torah, we "join" G-d, as it were, and leave this world too.

By being part of G-d's Torah, we actually connect to the spiritual world in a very direct and real way. Where is G-d right now? Well, G-d is above time and is not limited by time or space. So G-d is part of history, He is with you right now reading this book, and He's in the future sitting with the Mashiach right now as well! So by learning Torah, you can access a world that is above time too. By studying Torah, explains the Talmud, we are, so to speak, bringing G-d's Presence into this world.[219]

> Torah is the thought process of G-d—it's His will for this world.

The Torah allows us to understand G-d's Mind, which means His Will for Creation. That's an other-worldly ability, and it merits bringing the Mashiach too.

---

219   *Berachos* 6a.

Chapter Fifteen

WHAT WE SAY IS KEEPING US IN EXILE

OF ALL THE negative mitzvos in the Torah, *lashon hara*, destructive speech about other people, is considered one of the worst things a person can do. It's so bad that the Talmud states that speaking negatively about others is equivalent to performing the three cardinal sins of Jewish law — idolatry, sexual immorality, and murder. *Lashon hara* is equivalent in severity to them all![220]

In order to understand why negative speech is judged so harshly, we need to understand the power of positive speech.

The Mishnah tells us that G-d created the world using ten statements.[221] This means that in the course of the narrative describing the creation of the world in *Bereishis*, after the initial statement of Creation, "*Bereishis bara* — In the beginning of G-d's Creation," the words "and G-d said" are mentioned nine times.[222] For example:

- "G-d said, let there be light"[223]
- "G-d said, Let there be a firmament and let it divide the waters"[224]

---

220   Talmud Yerushalmi, *Peah* 1:1.
221   *Pirkei Avos* 5:1.
222   *Bereishis* 1:1.
223   Ibid. v. 3.
224   Ibid. v. 6.

- "G-d said, Let the waters be gathered, and let the dry land appear"[225]

Although the Torah's description of Creation is considered one of the most esoteric parts of the entire Torah, on a simple level we can see that speech is a faculty that has the power to create. How does G-d notify us of the awesome power that lies in speech? By informing us that He used speech to make all of Creation. All the trees, mountains, animals, heaven and earth, and the entire universe came into existence because of the speech that G-d used to create them.

HUMANS ARE SPEAKERS

If that's true for G-d, it's also true for us.

We humans are unique in Creation in that we have the ability to communicate through speech. Different animals have incredible ways to communicate between themselves through dance, smell, wing movement, or many other ways. Humans were created with the ability to speak. Actually, in a number of ancient Jewish sources, humans are referred to as the *medaber*, the speaker.[226] It's the faculty of speech more than anything else that distinguishes us from the animal kingdom, and in turn reflects the difference in essence between the humans and the animal kingdom, with which we may have a number of things in common, such as eating, sleeping, and reproducing. However, intrinsically humans are speakers, and thereby live on a higher plane of existence. We are the *medaber*.

If G-d used speech to create the world, then we humans who possess the faculty of speech can build the world with the power of our speech too. And if positive speech can build, then negative speech can destroy — whether we are aware of it or not. Speaking *lashon hara* can have fatal consequences on the lives of others. By saying things that can damage another person's livelihood, family, or reputation, one is

---

225   Ibid. v. 9.
226   Onkelos on *Bereishis* 2:7 translates the words "*Ha-adam l'nefesh chayah*," man became a living being, to "*V'havat b'adam l'ruach memalala*," man became a speaking being.

acting in the exact opposite way to how G-d wants you to act. G-d wants us to become partners in the continuation of the Creation of the World. G-d began Creation with speech and now expects us to continue this Creation by using this unique human faculty to build up the world around us. By hurting people with our words, we are going against everything G-d expects of us as humans. Using our words for strife, argument, and gossip, we are breaking down the world order and bringing destruction to an otherwise beautiful world.

> Torah is the thought process of G-d — it's His will for this world.

There's more: Speech is directly connected to our possessing the Land of Israel in peace, and even to reducing the amount of time we have to wait for the Final Redemption. Let's understand this deep idea by examining a famous episode from the Torah that involved negative speech and prevented us from being redeemed.

THE SPIES ENTER THE LAND

Negative speech prevented the entire Jewish people from entering the Land of Israel at the appointed time. Soon after leaving Egypt and receiving the Torah, G-d told the Jewish people it was time to prepare for entering the Land of Israel. Entering Israel was the reason they were taken out of Egypt in the first place, and the giving of the Torah outside of Israel was to prepare them to perform the mitzvos in Israel. However, the Torah tells us that the Jewish people became fearful of entering the Land and wanted to send in spies to see what they would be up against once they did enter.

Appointing spies was seen as a lack of faith by G-d and Moshe Rabbeinu, however G-d acquiesced to their demands and permitted Moshe Rabbeinu to select the best men for the job. Twelve leaders, one from each tribe, were chosen. After surveying the Land in forty days and seeing the size and power of the people who were inhabiting it, ten of the twelve came back with a very negative report, and said, "We cannot ascend to the Land to drive out that people, for it is too strong for us!" They announced an evil report to the Children of Israel regarding the Land that they had spied, saying, "The Land through which we have passed is a land that devours its inhabitants! All the people that we saw there were huge…we were like grasshoppers in their eyes!"[227]

The Spies Speak Badly about the Land

The job was done. The people lost all hope in their ability to successfully enter the Land, even though it was promised to them by G-d Himself and they had the great leadership of Moshe Rabbeinu, Aaron, Miriam, and others to bring them in. Their fear was understandable — the Land was filled with much more powerful nations — however, how they reacted to that reality was the problem: They stayed up all night and cried, as it says, "The entire assembly raised up and issued its voice, the people wept that night."[228] This demonstrated their absolute lack of faith in G-d and His chosen leader Moshe Rabbeinu: "Why is G-d bringing us to this Land to die by the sword? Our wives and young children will be taken captive! Is it not better for us to return to Egypt? So they said to one another, 'Let us appoint a leader and let us return to Egypt!'"[229]

The national hysteria that ensued became one of the most tragic points of Jewish history. The negative ripple effect of that night is still felt today. Since they didn't want to go in, G-d punished them by not permitting them to enter. That entire generation that left Egypt died in the desert and only their children were permitted to enter. That explains why they had to wander in the desert for forty years, which was enough time for that generation to pass. Only those who were young enough when they left Egypt to not be held culpable for the sin of the Spies were permitted to enter.

What exactly did they do wrong? They were scared, and rightly so, but they did something inexcusable along the way: they spoke negatively about the Land itself. The Talmud tells us that the decree that the Jewish people had to wander in the desert for forty years was sealed due to the *lashon hara* the spies spoke and the fact that the Jewish people believed what they said regarding the Land of Israel, as it says, "They

---

227   *Bamidbar* 13:31.
228   Ibid. 14:1.
229   Ibid. v. 3–4.

brought forth to the Children of Israel an evil report on the Land that they had spied out."[230] This, says the Chafetz Chaim, was what sealed their fate, kept them in exile, and prevented them from entering the Land. By speaking *lashon hara*, one not only gets removed from the Land, but one loses one's right to enter it.

We are still feeling the repercussions of that fateful night. The Sages tell us that the date of the night they cried about entering the Land was Tishah b'Av, the ninth day of the Jewish month of Av. That date has become synonymous with the Jewish people being exiled from the Land in the time of the destruction of the First and Second Temples, and many other calamities besides that.[231]

It's true for them and it's true for us too. Speaking derogatory and destructive speech about others prolongs the exile and prevents the coming of the Mashiach. Even speaking about an inanimate object like the Land of Israel itself is considered a terrible sin for which exile is deserved;[232] how much more so does saying derogative and destructive speech about other people keep us in exile and prevent the redemption of the Jewish people by the Mashiach!

THE FIVE FORMS OF FORBIDDEN SPEECH

Negative speech comes in five categories. By avoiding these five, we have a much better chance of bringing peace to the world and the eventual redemption of our people. Here are the five forms:

1. *Rechilus* — **Harmful Gossip:** This refers to gossip spoken about what a third party said about the listener: "Do you know what

---

230   Ibid. 13:32.

231   The original exile of mankind from the Garden of Eden was also a result of them believing the slander of the snake against G-d in terms of His motivations for forbidding them to eat from the Tree of Knowledge.

232   The Talmud in *Kesubos* 112b states that Rabbi Chanina would repair any potholes he would encounter in Israel so that travelers would not fall and consequently speak ill of the Land of Israel. Rabbi Ammi and Rabbi Asi would stand and pass from a sunny spot to a shady one, and from a shady spot to a sunny one, so that they would always sit in comfort and never have cause to remark that they were uncomfortable in the Land of Israel.

Sarah said about you?" or "Do you know what Harry did to you?"[233]

2. *Lashon Hara* — **Harmful or Derogatory Speech**: Truthful but damaging speech about another person or business falls under this category: "Don't shop in Dan's store; he's a little weird," or "Don't eat in that restaurant; the waitress was not nice to me."[234]

3. *Motzi Shem Ra* — **Untrue Derogatory Speech**: This is untrue and potentially derogatory speech: "Don't date him; I heard he served time in prison for tax fraud."[235]

4. *Ona'as Devarim* — **Painful Speech**: Embarrassing someone, cursing at him, shouting at him, or any type of speech that causes harm to another person all constitute *ona'as devarim*.[236]

5. *Avak Lashon Hara* — **(literally, "dust or particles of *lashon hara*") derogatory speech, close to *lashon hara*:** These are comments you make that could be understood in different ways. "Wow, my neighbor's refrigerator is always full." This could be understood as a compliment, that the family is always ready for guests, or it could be an insult, that they are gluttonous.[237]

By refraining from these five categories we have a higher chance of creating a better environment for the eventual Mashiach and the building of the Temple in Yerushalayim.

---

233   Among other things, this may cause the listener to retaliate against the speaker.

234   It is not fair to judge the place and tell people not to eat there based on one incident with a waitress.

235   We learn from here that it is forbidden to tell a lie.

236   All speech, whether true or false, that upsets another person falls under this category.

237   These comments are the least problematic of the five, but we are still told to be careful in avoiding such statements for they can be construed to be negative by the listener.

Chapter Sixteen

THE MASHIACH AND HIS UNEXPECTED ARRIVAL

THE COMING OF the Mashiach can occur in one of two forms: He can be ushered in with great miracles, the likes of which have not been experienced since the Exodus from Egypt under Moshe Rabbeinu, or in a more prosaic manner. These two possible miraculous scenarios are featured in words of the Prophets.

The prophet Daniel was one of two people aware of when the End of Days would occur and yet was prevented by G-d from revealing it. In the Book of Daniel we are told, "I was watching in night visions and behold! With the clouds of heavens, one like a man came; he came up to the Ancient of Days, and they brought him before Him. He gave him dominion, honor, and languages will serve him; his dominion is everlasting and will not pass, and his kingship will not be destroyed."[238]

The imagery of "clouds of heavens" used by the prophet informs us that the Mashiach will come suddenly and with great heavenly support.

The second scenario is given to us by the prophet Zechariah,[239] "Behold, your king comes to you...humble and riding upon a donkey." Not so exciting.

Well, which one is it? Will he come with exciting miracles or in a mundane fashion? Rabbi Yehoshua ben Levi tells us that these two

---

238   *Daniel* 7:13–14.
239   *Zechariah* 9:9.

prophetic accounts are not contradictory versions, but two alternatives: "If the Jewish people merit it, he will come with the clouds, but if they do not merit it, he will appear poor and riding upon a donkey."[240]

These two alternatives may also differ in the timing of the delivery too. We have two possible dates for the coming of the Mashiach: the outside time and the earlier time. The outside time is the six thousandth year from Creation, and will occur whether we deserve it or not. The earlier time, however, can happen at any moment if we deserve the redemption.

These two scenarios revealed to us by Daniel and Zechariah may actually be explanations of these two dates if we include the words of the prophet Yeshayah as the resolving prophecy: "The smallest will increase a thousand-fold, and the youngest into a mighty nation, in its time, I will hasten it."[241]

This last expression is worth examining. "In its time" in Hebrew is *b'ito*; "I will hasten it" in Hebrew is *achishenah*. Which is it? In its time or hastened?

It seems as though Yeshayah was seeing contradictory visions, and yet they appear in the same verse! However, the Gemara explains that if we connect this prophecy together with those of Daniel and Zechariah, the full picture emerges: If we merit it, G-d will hasten the Redemption (*achishenah*) and bring us our long-awaited Mashiach on a cloud of miracles and splendor. If, however, we do not merit the early intervention of the Mashiach, we are still guaranteed of his arrival, but that will occur at the end of the six thousand years (*b'ito*), and it will not come with splendid miracles, but with a more mundane and earthly arrival of the Mashiach on his donkey.

Why was the imagery of a donkey transporting the newly revealed Mashiach used as a metaphor as opposed to any other animal? Why not a strong horse or a fast camel?

The donkey is a faithful animal, yet slow-moving and a rather sluggish

---

240   *Sanhedrin* 98a.
241   *Yeshayah* 60:22.

creature. This represents the less miraculous method of the Mashiach's arrival. And, by examining the Hebrew word for a donkey, *chamor*, we have another insight into the Mashiach's later arrival.

The word *chamor* is related to another Hebrew word, *chomer*, which means physicality. The donkey represents the idea of the more physical aspects of Creation as opposed to the more spiritual and elevated ones. So if we are not able to merit the Redemption at an earlier stage through our spiritual actions, the Mashiach will come to us riding on a donkey, meaning on the backs of our less spiritual and more physical actions. If we don't merit miracles, our salvation will come in the form of the Mashiach arriving on a humble donkey rather than an ostentatious horse as he enters the gates of Yerushalayim.

This, however, is no ordinary donkey. That same donkey on which Avraham rode, taking Yitzchak to the *Akeidah*, and Moshe Rabbeinu later rode on his mission to Egypt, will be the donkey on which the Mashiach will ride on in the future.[242]

LIKE FINDING SOMETHING OR A SCORPION BITE

A basic tenet of the Jewish faith is that the Mashiach can arrive at any moment without any warning.

Rabbi Zeira in the Talmud found a group of great rabbis in a discussion attempting to predict when the Mashiach will come. He became very passionate about the discussion and said, "Please! I beg you not to delay the coming of the Mashiach, because it is known that three things come to us quickly and without warning, and they are the Mashiach, finding something you've been looking for, and a scorpion."[243]

> The Mashiach can arrive at any moment without any warning.

What is it about a scorpion and finding something you've been looking for that Rabbi Zeira felt he needed to compare them to the coming of the Mashiach? A scorpion bites without any warning, and finding

---

242   *Pirkei D'Rebbi Eliezer* 31.
243   *Sanhedrin* 97a.

something you've been looking for happens when you least expect it. So too, the Mashiach's arrival can come at any given moment. The Maharsha adds an interesting connection to something we've already discussed, and that is the two ways the Mashiach can come. If we are meritorious, the Mashiach will arrive in a miraculous and painless fashion, without much suffering, like the feeling of finding something you've been looking for. However if we are not meritorious, the Mashiach's arrival will come with much suffering very much like a scorpion's bite.

In order for the Mashiach to be able to come at any moment, there must be a potential candidate ready at all times to serve the function of the Mashiach. In every generation since the destruction of the Temple, there has lived a very great individual of outstanding piety ready to take on the mantle of leadership to become the Mashiach. This individual is not aware of his mission as the redeemer until the appointed time of the Redemption arrives. This is very much like the great redeemer Moshe Rabbeinu who was not aware of his unique role of redeeming the Jewish people from Egypt until much later in life. G-d in His infinite wisdom kept the fact that Moshe Rabbeinu was going to be the one to go into Egypt and act as G-d's redeemer secret even from Moshe Rabbeinu himself.

The Talmud tells us the story of one such man who had the merit of meeting the potential Mashiach. The conversation he had with him is recorded in the Talmud. Let's meet this man and find out what exactly transpired.

THE MAN WHO MET THE MASHIACH

What would you ask the Mashiach if you met him on the street?

Well that happened, according to the Talmud, to a great Jewish scholar by the name of Rabbi Yehoshua ben Levi:[244]

> *Rabbi Yehoshua ben Levi met Eliyahu HaNavi at the entrance to a certain cave in Israel and took the opportunity to ask him whether he knew when the Mashiach was arriving. Eliyahu told him to ask the Mashiach himself!*

---

244   Ibid. 98a.

"Well, where is he?" he asked him. Eliyahu responded that he could find the Mashiach sitting at the gate of the city.[245]

Before Rabbi Yehoshua ben Levi left, he asked Eliyahu how he could recognize the Mashiach. Eliyahu responded, "He is the one sitting among the paupers afflicted with disease as they tie and untie their bandages."

So the rabbi went to search for the Mashiach. Upon finding him, the rabbi gave the Mashiach a very respectful greeting, "Peace be upon you my master and my teacher."

The Mashiach responded, "Peace be upon you, son of Levi."

Rabbi Yehoshua ben Levi grabbed the opportunity to ask him, "When is the master coming?"

The Mashiach answered him, "Today!"

Upon hearing this incredible news, the rabbi ran back to report his conversation with Eliyahu HaNavi.

"What did he tell you?" asked Eliyahu.

"Well, first of all he greeted me by referring to me as the 'son of Levi.'"

Eliyahu responded to this by saying, "This is a sign that you and your father are destined for the Next World." (The fact that he greeted him at all, says Rashi, proves that both the rabbi and his father who was referenced were going to inherit the Next World.)

Rabbi Yehoshua ben Levi said to Eliyahu, "But he spoke falsely to me! He told me that he would arrive today, and he didn't come."

"You misunderstood," responded Eliyahu. "He said he would arrive today, as in the verse, 'Today, if you heed His voice.'"[246]

---

245 The Vilna Gaon amends this text to read that the gate of the city is actually a reference to the gate of Rome. We will see the significance of Rome and Christianity in the advent of the Mashiach later on in this book.

246 *Tehillim* 95:7.

What did Rabbi Yehoshua ben Levi misunderstand in the words of the Mashiach? Eliyahu explained to Rabbi Yehoshua ben Levi the true meaning of the Mashiach's word "today" as a reference to the sentiment so powerfully expressed by David HaMelech to the Jewish people. He truthfully stated that he is poised, willing, and able to arrive at any moment. However, it is up to us, the Jewish people, to heed G-d's voice in order to merit the great change to the world that the Mashiach will bring.

DON'T ATTEMPT TO PREDICT THE TIME OF MASHIACH'S ARRIVAL

It appears from the Talmudic piece we looked at before that Rabbi Zeira had a problem with the rabbis attempting to predict the exact time of the Mashiach's arrival. His reasoning was that when the predicted date arrives, people will expect the Mashiach to come specifically at that time. If the prediction was off, which has happened on numerous occasions throughout Jewish history, people would lose hope in the Mashiach coming at all. This could lead to people losing faith in the G-d of the Jewish people too, and that itself could delay the coming of the Mashiach.

DON'T JUST WAIT FOR THE MASHIACH — ANTICIPATE HIS ARRIVAL

One of the questions the Talmud tells us we will be asked once we move into the next world is, "Did you anticipate the arrival of the Mashiach?"[247] From this and from the words of the Rambam in his list of the Thirteen Principles of Jewish Faith, we are expected to believe and anticipate the arrival of the Mashiach at any given moment, "I believe with a perfect faith in the coming of the Mashiach. And even though he tarries, I shall expect his arrival every single day."

From here we see that just waiting for the Mashiach isn't enough, we must pray for his arrival, and we must anticipate his imminent arrival

---

247   *Shabbos* 31a.

too. According to Rabbi Yitzchak Zev Soloveitchik, this means we must be able to say that the Mashiach can come at any given moment and we anticipate his arrival with a full heart.[248]

This is why our daily prayers make reference to our desire for the Mashiach to come. In the *Shemoneh Esrei*, the standing prayer we recite three times a day in the morning, afternoon, and evening, the paragraph for the coming of the Mashiach was instituted and given a set wording: "The offspring of Your servant David, may You speedily cause to flourish, and enhance his pride through Your salvation, for we hope for Your salvation all day long. Blessed are You, Hashem, Who causes the pride of salvation to flourish."

So three times a day we ask G-d to shorten the exile and to bring the Mashiach to redeem us.

CHEVLEI MASHIACH: BIRTH PAINS OF THE MASHIACH

A number of metaphors are used in the Talmud to describe the period before the Mashiach arrives.[249] One of the metaphors used to describe the dawn of the Mashiach's arrival is *chevlei Mashiach*, the birth pains of the Mashiach. What can we learn about the pre-Messianic era from this unusual expression? The comparison, says the Chafetz Chaim, is because the prelude to the Mashiach is very much like the pain a woman experiences before and during childbirth.[250] Let's examine the nine-month journey a woman goes through before giving birth to see why.

The Redemption, says the Vilna Gaon, is referred to as morning.[251] This is based on the words of the prophet Yeshayah, "Morning has come, as well as night."[252] Likewise, Yeshayah also refers to it as a birth when he says, "For Zion has had contractions and has even given birth."[253]

---

248   Rabbi Yitzchak Zev Soloveitchik, *Likutei HaGriz*, vol. 2, pg. 81.
249   *Shabbos* 118a.
250   Chafetz Chaim, *Shem Olam* 12.
251   Vilna Gaon, *Even Sheleimah* 11.
252   *Yeshayah* 21:12.
253   Ibid. 66:8.

The darkest time of night is that which precedes the dawn, and the strongest labor pains are those immediately preceding the moment of birth. So it will be before the Redemption. The final exile will be the most intense of all the exiles.

> The final exile will be the most intense of all the exiles.

At first, the news of the prospective baby is very exciting. As the months go by, the discomfort starts to increase, at first with mild pains, and eventually with heavier and heavier ones. As the woman reaches the final weeks, the pain becomes very great, and this itself is an indication of the readiness of the baby to appear. It's at this point that the woman begins to wonder whether the child will ever come out! The days before birth are the most intense — the mother can hardly sleep, eat, or walk normally — and is preoccupied with one thing only: When am I going to finally give birth?

Finally, after many months, the moment arrives. What seemed like a never-ending process happens in the blink of an eye. Very few moments of a person's life take one from such extreme pain and hopelessness to ecstatic joy in such a short period of time. The child emerges and the miracle of birth happens before our very eyes. What seemed impossible has just become real. From living in liquid for nine months, the baby immediately adapts to its new environment and begins breathing air for the very first time. A child is born.

The Messianic era, we are told, will follow a very similar pattern. Before the Redemption begins, the pain and suffering will go from bad to worse. Every day the physical and spiritual pain will only increase until all we will be able to say is, "When is this going to stop?" Actually, according to the Talmud, one of the signs that the end is near is when you see a generation of Jews suffering like a river washing over them.[254] That's a sign we are close.

The comparison goes even deeper. The Talmud tells us that the Son of David will not arrive until a foreign kingdom will have extended its dominion over Israel for nine months. This is based on the words of

---

254 *Sanhedrin* 98a.

Michah the Prophet who says, "Therefore He will surrender them until the time that one who gives birth has given birth; then the rest of his brothers will return with the Children of Israel."[255] This means that G-d will surrender the Jewish people to their enemies for the length of time that a woman bears a child — nine months. After this nine-month period of challenge, the rest of the Jewish people will unite together in the Land of Israel.

So challenging will those times be that some of the Sages in the Talmud tell us that they anticipated the coming Redeemer but prayed that they would not see him.[256] Although they prayed for his arrival, they didn't want to be a part of this final period of Jewish history. However, as we shall soon see, we have the ability to reduce any pain and suffering during this period if we are careful to be involved in a number of spiritual activities.

SOCIETY DISINTEGRATES

The pain and the suffering experienced by the generation before the Mashiach comes may be the symptoms of the world's decline that must necessarily precede the Messianic Era. The Talmud describes this state of affairs when Rabbi Yitzchak said to Rabbi Nachman, "This is what Rabbi Yochanan said: In the generation when the Son of David (the Mashiach) will come, the number of Torah scholars will decrease. And as for the rest of the people, their eyes will become worn out through grief and anxiety. Numerous troubles and harsh decrees will constantly be appearing anew."[257]

Abarbanel explains that this suffering and the subsequent breakdown of society will make way for a new era.[258] For this to happen and to allow for the profound and comprehensive change that the Messianic era will bring, the current norms and values must collapse.

---

255   *Michah* 5:2.
256   *Sanhedrin* 98b.
257   Ibid. 97a.
258   Abarbanel, *Yeshuos Meshicho, Iyun* 1, chap. 5.

Part of this will be a wave of atheism that will sweep throughout the world and even the Jewish people before the Messianic era. This will be remedied by the Mashiach's arrival, says Abarbanel, as the prophet Yeshayah says, "The earth will be filled with the knowledge of Hashem as water covering the seabed."[259] This stands in contrast to the pre-Messianic era where the world will see a dearth of knowledge of G-d. This is also what Rabbi Yochanan meant above when he said, "The number of Torah scholars will decrease."

Another contrast will be the joy and happiness that will accompany the Mashiach's arrival. As the prophet Yeshayah says, "For in gladness shall you go out, and in peace shall you arrive." Additionally, he says, "I will rejoice intensely with Hashem, my soul will exalt with my G-d."[260] However, in the pre-Messianic era, as the Talmud told us above, "Their eyes will become worn out through grief and anxiety."

SEVENTY YEARS AND THE LAST FORTY-FIVE DAYS OF THE EXILE

According to the Vilna Gaon, these birth pains will last seventy years.[261] Just as in Egypt the oppression increased prior to the Redemption, as it says, "Let the work be heavier upon the men,"[262] so will it be in the period of the birth pangs of Mashiach. The seventy words in Psalm 20 parallel the seventy years of the birth pangs of Mashiach from which the Jewish people will be redeemed.

Of the entire redemptive process, the last forty-five days will be the most challenging. These last days will propel the Jewish people to do complete repentance and will allow us to merit the Final Redemption. According to Rabbi Avraham Azulai: "The troubles shall increase as they never did before…these are the forty-five days in the future when Israel will go out of Yerushalayim to be in the desert of the nations of the

---

259   *Yeshayah* 11:9.
260   Ibid. 55:12, 61:10.
261   Vilna Gaon, *Even Sheleimah* 11.
262   *Shemos* 5:9.

world, just as Lot was displaced during the upheaval of Sodom when he was not able to save even a small piece of bread and he was rushed out into the desert. Actually, the troubles of the Jewish people will be in a very similar manner. The Jewish people will be dispersed throughout the desert."[263]

Why does there need to be such a challenging time before the arrival of the Mashiach? Why do so many travails need to present themselves?

Rabbi Elchanan Wasserman explains this in a small book called *Ikvesa DeMeshicha* and says, "Since with the coming of the Mashiach the world will be in a perfected, flawless state, it is necessary for all old accounts to be settled in the period that precedes it. Piles of accounts have accumulated in heaven from the time of Creation to the present (that is, sins that man has not yet rectified), and they must be put in order before the Mashiach comes. It is therefore the duty of every individual to pay what he still owes to heaven."[264]

The *Chesed L'Avraham* writes that the intensification of Israel's oppression constitutes a challenging process of purification in preparation for the Redemption:

> *The Jewish people's challenges will become very difficult and they will suffer intense pain. They will say of the mountains, "They have covered us," and of the hills, "They have fallen upon us," because of the tremendous troubles that will surround them on all sides. The reason for this is that the Divine Presence will judge its household, and G-d will bring them back to the established covenant so as to purify them for the Redemption and for the goodness promised to us by His prophets.*
>
> *That goodness is something the intellect cannot comprehend. The redemption from Egypt and its accompanying miracles will pale in comparison with the miracles and wonders that will happen to us during the redemption of Israel at the End*

---

263   Rabbi Avraham Azulai, *Chesed L'Avraham* 5:35.
264   Rabbi Elchanan Wasserman, *Ikvesa D'Meshicha* 18.

of Days. As it says, "They will no longer say, 'By the Life of Hashem Who brought the Children of Israel up from the Land of Egypt,' but instead, 'By the life of Hashem Who brought up and brought back the descendants of the House of Israel from the northern land and from all the lands to which He dispersed them.'"[265]

There will then be miracles and revelation of the Divine Presence to Israel in an amazingly wondrous fashion. All who merit those times will say, "Behold, this is our G-d in Whom we placed our hopes,"[266] literally pointing a finger at the revelation of the Divine Presence. Who will be worthy of this?[267]

According to Rabbi Yaakov Yisrael Kanievsky, although we cannot determine when the birth pains of Mashiach actually begin or end, we know that we are currently near the end, as the bulk was experienced by the Jewish people during the Second World War.[268]

The *Ohr HaChaim* suggests that all these travails of the pre-Messianic era will only occur in the event that the Mashiach comes without our positively meriting him.[269] Should we bring the Redemption through studying Torah and performing mitzvos, the Mashiach's arrival will not be preceded by suffering. Our failing to do so will potentially lead to a leader who wishes to destroy us, much like Haman from the story of Purim.

HOW CLOSE ARE WE TO THE MASHIACH'S ARRIVAL?

The Chafetz Chaim was considered the spiritual leader of his day by Jews throughout the world. His works are studied to this very day with great devotion and respect. He died in 1933 and even had an obituary written about him in the *New York Times*. Before he died, he wrote a number of things about the advent of the Messianic era, which he felt

---

265   *Yirmiyah* 23:7–8.

266   *Yeshayah* 25:9.

267   *Chesed L'Avraham* 1:17.

268   Rabbi Yaakov Yisrael Kanievsky, *Orchos Rabbeinu*, vol. 1, pg. 287.

269   *Bereishis* 49:11.

was very close. He wrote, "We should hope that G-d doesn't keep the exile going much longer, because our physical and spiritual powers are weakening. You should know that we have passed the official time of his arrival, and are right before the birth of a new era."[270] This, says the Chafetz Chaim, is very much like the end of the Egyptian exile. Even though the time of redemption had come, the servitude and pain of the Egyptian slavery increased until they were able to leave.

However, one should not focus on the exact time of the Final Redemption. The Chafetz Chaim was against this, saying, "We cannot know the precise time of the Final Redemption. Because when the Holy One, Blessed Be He, openly revealed the end of the Babylonian exile and said that it would last seventy years, even then many calculated the time incorrectly. How much more so the Final Redemption, which is even more hidden! However, from the level of our distress we can understand that it will not be that much longer."[271]

The Talmud goes as far as to curse any person who attempts to calculate the precise time of the Mashiach's arrival. The *Akeidas Yitzchak* explains why:

> *When G-d has said in Yeshayah, "The day of vengeance is in My heart,"*[272] *He means that He will not reveal the timing but it remains in His heart. This is why the Talmud curses those who calculate the timing of the Mashiach's arrival beforehand. Such calculations actually delay his arrival. If someone had calculated that the Mashiach would not arrive until the year seven thousand using astronomic and astrological data, we would resign ourselves to a lengthy exile and slacken our efforts to hasten his arrival through the performance of good deeds.*
>
> *We must believe that "My redemption is close at hand,"*[273] *and that when least thought about, it may arrive. Experience has*

---

270   Chafetz Chaim, *Shem Olam* 12.

271   Ibid., part 2.

272   *Yeshayah* 63:4.

273   Ibid. 56:1.

taught us that G-d may hasten the end, when He shortened our exile in Egypt. "I the Lord, at its time, I will hasten it."[274] G-d reserves the right to accelerate His timetable, if warranted. We learn from here that "natural law" can be supplanted by hashgachah pratis, G-d's direct involvement.[275]

HOW LONG WILL THE MESSIANIC ERA LAST?

Once the Mashiach arrives, how long will the entire Messianic era last? A number of different answers are given to this question, varying in lengths of time from forty years to a thousand years or more.

- According to Rabbi Eliezer in the Talmud, the Messianic period will last forty years.[276] It's after this amount of time that the period of the Resurrection of the Dead will begin. (We will examine the period of resurrection later in this book.) Rabbi Eliezer sees an allusion to this amount of time in *Sefer Tehillim*, "For forty years I shall take a generation."[277] The future tense of the word "take," *akut*, and the idea of a future generation is a reference to a very different and unique generation that, says the Talmud, is the Messianic one. So these forty years will come as a preparation for the Resurrection of the Dead.
- Another opinion in the same piece of Talmud is that the Messianic era will last seventy years, while the great leader Rabbi Yehudah HaNasi, Judah the Prince, says it will last three generations.
- According to the Rambam, the Mashiach, who is a regular man of flesh and blood, will die after a lengthy reign and will be succeeded by a son and then a grandson.[278] By specifying three generations, the Rambam is implying that the Messianic

---

274   Ibid. 60:22.
275   *Akeidas Yitzchak* 56:15.
276   *Sanhedrin* 99a.
277   *Tehillim* 95:10.
278   Rambam, commentary to the Mishnah, introduction to the eleventh chapter of *Sanhedrin*.

dynasty will not endure any longer than three generations before the Resurrection of the Dead begins.

- Still another opinion in the same Talmud discussion says that according to Rabbi Dosa, the Messianic era will last four hundred years.

- Another version of Rabbi Yehudah HaNasi's opinion is that the Messianic era will last three hundred and sixty-five years, and a final opinion of Avimi is that the Messianic era will last seven thousand years!

ADVANCED TECHNOLOGY IN THE MESSIANIC ERA

Many traditions predict that there will be an extremely advanced technology in the Messianic era. The prophet Yeshayah alluded to this when he said, "Then the eyes of the blind will be opened and the ears of the deaf will be opened. Then the lame will skip like a gazelle and the tongue of the mute shall sing glad song."[279] Some understand these words metaphorically and say that the blind and mute people Yeshayah is talking about is a description of the downtrodden Jewish people who have been through countless exiles and persecutions and have become blind to the truth and deaf to those that try to encourage them.

Others, however, understand the words of the prophet literally. People who were blind and deaf will begin seeing again and hearing again during the Messianic period. The Midrash says that this verse applies to the true future world of *Olam Haba* and is a reference to the world after the Resurrection of the Dead.[280] G-d will firstly bring the dead back to life with the particular ailments they suffered from when they were alive and only then will He heal them. This seems to indicate that the healing will come in the form of miracles performed by G-d as opposed to any advanced medical technology.

---

279 *Yeshayah* 35:5–6.
280 *Bereishis Rabbah* 95:1.

However, we have already spoken about the view of those such as Shmuel and Rabbi Gamliel in the Talmud (and eventually the Rambam) who say the miracles of the Messianic era will not involve any change in the laws of nature. When discussing miracles, the Rambam makes a statement that any type of miracle can only produce a temporary result.[281] Since the restoration of sight and hearing, plus the myriad of other diseases such as cancer, heart disease, and the like will be eliminated forever, it must be that all disease will be cured through natural means — an advanced technology of which we are seeing today happen across the world, and in particular in the technological medical advancements coming from Israel itself. Interestingly, Israel is at the forefront of incredible cures for diseases that our ancestors could only dream about.

CONQUERING WORLD HUNGER

In addition to the medical advances, much has been predicted and written on the agricultural changes we will see leading up to and during the Messianic era. A number of changes in the nature of the agricultural world are discussed, such as grapes as large as the hen's eggs, and grains of wheat as big as a fist. The amount of labor that will be needed to process agricultural products will be greatly reduced to the point that clothing and loaves of bread will seem to grow on trees.

In addition, the knowledge and understanding of how trees produce fruits will increase so dramatically that trees will be able to bear fruit continually. The Talmud relates that Rabban Gamliel discussed these predictions with his students.[282] When one of the students scoffed at the idea of a plant bringing out new fruits every day, Rabbi Gamliel didn't just say, "Well, it's a miracle." Instead, he took the young man out to see a certain plant called the caper bush, which is a low, prickly, shrub native to the Mediterranean regions that had three edible parts, and would grow in quick succession.

---

281   *Iggeres Techi'as HaMeisim* of the Rambam, pg. 19, cited in Rabbi Aryeh Kaplan, *Immortality, Resurrection, and Age of the Universe* (Ktav Publishing), pg. 38.

282   *Shabbos* 30b.

Even the Land of Israel will have a different quality once the Mashiach comes, and will produce ready-made bread and fine wool clothes. Again, most people understand this metaphorically and say that this does not mean bread will be rising out of the ground, but rather technology will be at such a level people will be able to produce food and clothing for themselves without any hardship whatsoever so that it will seem as though the earth is producing them on its own.

What is the purpose of all these changes in the world, and why are they necessary for the period of the Mashiach? All of these advancements will occur for a number of reasons. Among them is so that people will be able to recognize G-d's greatness in a more palpable fashion. In addition, the comfort that comes with such an easy life will ultimately allow people to use their free time to be involved in spiritual pursuits and to achieve spiritual perfection.

THE WOLF LIVING WITH THE SHEEP — LITERAL OR METAPHORIC?

According to the Rambam, the main difference between before and after the Mashiach arrives will be that the Jews will no longer be subjugated and persecuted by the other nations. This peacefulness will eventually be felt by the entire world. Yeshayah describes this time of universal peace in the following way: "The wolf will live with the sheep and the leopard will lie down with the kid; and a calf, a lion cub, and a fatling will walk together, and a young child will lead them. A cow and bear will graze and their young will lie down together; and a lion, like cattle, will eat straw."[283]

> The spirit of peace and tranquility will affect the animal kingdom.

Here, we are being introduced to the spirit of peace and tranquility that will pervade the world when the Mashiach comes. Whether these references to animals that traditionally are at odds with each other actually being peaceful with one another are metaphorical or not is a difference

283 *Yeshayah* 11:6–7.

of opinion among the Sages. According to some, this prophecy is literal, and refers to changes in the actual animal kingdom.[284]

Wild animals and domestic beasts will coexist in harmony as they did at the start of Creation in the Garden of Eden. One commentator takes this literally, but only in reference to the animals in the Land of Israel, which will change in their relationship to other animals, unlike animals that reside outside of Israel, which will remain the same.

According to the *Akeidas Yitzchak*, this will occur because "man survives only as a species, not as an individual. Nevertheless, performing just deeds, or dispensing justice, has the advantage that it enables civilization to function, removes violence, and prevents warfare by the strong against the weak. This brings in its wake the harmony that is the task of the Mashiach to establish, as outlined in the Book of Yeshayah,[285] which even leads to peaceful relations in the animal kingdom."[286] So according to him, the peace within the animal kingdom is an outgrowth of the peace that will exist among mankind, and is therefore literal.

However, the accepted view is that this discussion of beasts and animals living in harmony is actually a metaphor. The nature of animals will not actually change at all in the Messianic era. Those animals that are carnivores will remain so after the Mashiach comes, and they will continue to prey on other creatures for their survival. The metaphor being used here is to indicate that the nations of the world, which act like wild animals by devouring the smaller nations that they come upon, will cease their desire to destroy and attack those nations. These "wild animals" will finally live in peace with the Jewish people and not seek their destruction anymore. The Rambam adds that although these prophecies are metaphorical, only when these actual events occur will we finally understand exactly what the prophet was describing to us.

What will bring about this change in the nature of man and animal?

---

284   *Toras Kohanim* to *Vayikra* 26:6.
285   *Yeshayah*, chap. 11.
286   *Akeidas Yitzchak* 46:6.

The prophet answers this by saying, "They will neither injure nor destroy in all of My sacred mountain, for the earth will be filled with the knowledge of G-d as water covers the seabed." This "sacred mountain" is a reference to the entire Land of Israel, as it is considered to stand higher and taller than all surrounding lands. So once the knowledge of G-d will be so pervasive throughout the entire world, ignorance will be totally banished from the world. Once people are wise about G-d, and their mission in G-d's world, then all hatred, fighting, and war will immediately cease, says the Rambam.[287]

The metaphor of "water covering the seabed" was used because water of the sea is never-ending and does not cease for even a moment. The water of the sea covers all the mountains and valleys that exist on the floor of the ocean. So too, all the different mistakes and false beliefs of the pre-Messianic era will be totally forgotten when the Mashiach arrives. They will be drowned out of existence, never to be seen again. It will seem as if they were never there, and their existence was like a bad dream.

The promise of world peace given by Yeshayah — "They shall beat their swords into plowshares and their spears into pruning hooks; nation will not lift sword against nation and they will no longer study warfare"[288] — is etched onto a wall in the United Nations Plaza, opposite the headquarters of United Nations in New York City.

INGATHERING OF THE WORLD'S JEWS TO ISRAEL

According to the Rambam, one of the main jobs of the Mashiach will be to bring the Jews that are scattered around the four corners of the earth to live in the Land of Israel. As Yeshayah HaNavi says: "It shall be on that day that the Lord will once again show His Hand to acquire the remnant of His People, who

> The Mashiach will bring the Jews that are scattered around the earth to live in the Land of Israel.

---

287 Rambam, *Moreh Nevuchim* 3:11.
288 *Yeshayah* 2:4.

will have remained from Assyria and from Egypt and from Pathos and from Cush and from Elam and from Shiner and from Hamath and from the islands of the sea. He will raise a banner for the nations and He will gather the lost of Israel, and He will gather in the dispersed ones of Yehudah from the four corners of the earth."[289]

Just as G-d redeemed the Jewish people from Egypt after hundreds of years of servitude before taking them to the promised Land of Israel, so too will G-d redeem the Jews from their lands and bring them to the Holy Land.

This process will actually begin before the Mashiach even arrives. The stage will be set for the Mashiach's arrival with Jews coming back to their land in droves. This may happen in one of two ways:

- The Jews will come voluntarily.
- They may flee the dangers of their countries in order to find a safe haven in the Land of Israel.

The Mashiach will merely complete this process by returning the "remnant" of the Jews from around the world.

If the Mashiach will bring Jews from all over the world, whether they are in China, Russia, France, Iran, the Dominican Republic, or wherever, why does Yeshayah need to mention the few locations as he does in the verse above? The answer is that there are two groups around the world today. Shortly after the death of Shlomo HaMelech, the Jews split into two groups. One was called the Northern Kingdom, which contained ten tribes who were exiled to a specific area. We do not know where these Jews are today, although experts speculate about different groups of Jews found in locations around the world who may be descendants of those of those original tribes. The remainder of the Jews from the southern part of Israel, the Kingdom of Yehudah, the Jews we are familiar with today, were dispersed throughout the entire world.

So the final ingathering of exiles will be total and complete — the ten tribes from the Northern Kingdom together with the dispersed of Yehudah.

---

289   Ibid. 11:11–12.

We are not sure exactly how G-d will bring about the initial ingathering of the exiles. It may be like the time of Cyrus when the Persian king encouraged the return of the Jews to the Land of Israel and to build the Second Temple. Maybe international political considerations will cause the nations of the world to help and encourage the Jews to return to their land, or maybe it will happen without international will. Only time will tell.

THE INGATHERING AND THE NUMBER FIVE

The ingathering of the Jewish people to Israel can be understood by examining the number five. The number five represents taking separate elements that are disparate and seemingly disconnected and uniting them through the central fifth point.

In order to understand how the number five represents this, we need to examine the number four. When we exist in this world, we are inside the number four. The world around us moves out into four directions. It was in four directions that the Jewish people were distributed during the four exiles, which represents being spread out all over the four directions of the world: north, south, east, and west.

The number five therefore represents the central fifth point that pulls all those four directions together — in this case, the return of the Jewish people from the four corners of the earth to the central location, Israel. Picture for yourself the side of a die that shows five dots. You'll notice that the four parts are on the extremes of the face; however, the fifth dot lies in the middle, pulling all the four dots together and creating a new unified reality, i.e., five. Five therefore represents the number of ingathering those disparate parts that were once spread out.

The transformation from four to five, from *galus*, exile, to *geulah*, redemption, can even be seen in the shape of the Hebrew letters as well. The shape of the *daled*, which is the fourth letter and represents the number four, contains two lines that extend to four directions on the horizontal and vertical axes. The fifth letter, *hey*, is made up of two letters — *daled* and a *yud* on the bottom-left corner. So the letter *hey* incorporates the four directions, but adds an additional *yud* that symbolizes the central fifth unifying point that joins the four directions together.

INTERSTELLAR FLIGHT

According to Rabbi Aryeh Kaplan, a master of mystical and esoteric Jewish writings, we can possibly see signs of interstellar flight being predicted in early Jewish writings.[290] The prophet Yeshayah writes, "Those whose hope is in Hashem will have renewed strength; they will grow a wing like eagles."[291] According to the *Zohar*, this is a reference to the advent of space flight.[292] In addition, the *Tikkunei Zohar* discusses interstellar colonization, as each righteous person will be given his own star to reside on.[293] We are not too sure what this means, but we are seeing today advances in space travel at an incredible pace. We even read in the news of the human colonization of Mars on a regular basis.

THE WELLSPRINGS OPEN

All of this technological advancement was predicted with uncanny accuracy by the *Zohar*. Some two thousand years ago, the *Zohar* states, "In the six hundredth year of the sixth millennium, the gates of wisdom on high and the wellsprings of lower wisdom will be opened. This will prepare the world to enter the seventh millennium, just as a man prepares himself towards sunset on Friday for the Sabbath."[294] This is a clear prediction that in the Jewish year 5600, which corresponds to the year 1840 CE, there will be a sudden explosion of worldly knowledge. Although nothing of note occurred in that precise year, that year does correspond to the onset of the present scientific revolution.

So advanced will the technology be that the true destructive powers of modern technology will create a generation that will have the power to destroy itself. This is hinted at in the words of Rabbi Eliezer when he says, "The Mashiach will come in a generation which is *ra'ui klia*," which means worthy of, or capable of, bringing about its own total

---

290   Rabbi Aryeh Kaplan, *Handbook of Jewish Thought* 24:8.
291   *Yeshayah* 40:31.
292   *Zohar* 1:12b.
293   *Tikkunei Zohar* 14b.
294   *Zohar* 1:117a.

destruction.[295] This can be understood as a reference to the devastating power of destruction we know exists in nuclear weapons.

The advanced state of technology that will come with the advent of the Messianic era will ultimately be used for the good. Every resource that exists on earth will be channeled for the improvement of mankind and the planet. Hunger, population problems, overcrowding, climate change, and a host of other challenges that plague society today will be gone. Whether this happens through natural or miraculous means is yet to be seen.

However, before or soon after the Mashiach's arrival, a great war has been predicted called the war of Gog and Magog. In the next chapter, we'll examine what that battle will really be all about.

---

295 End of *Pesikta Rabasi* 1.

Chapter Seventeen

THE FINAL WAR OF GOG AND MAGOG

BEFORE THE MASHIACH appears, or perhaps once he does reveal himself, a final war will take place in the Land of Israel. The Midrash tells us that there will be great suffering before the advent of the Messianic era. We are thus taught, "One-third of the world's woes will come in the generation before the Mashiach."[296] Yechezkel the Prophet describes this war as the battle of Gog and Magog,[297] as does Zechariah.[298] This battle will take place in the early days of the Messianic era, when the nations of the world led by Gog, king of Magog, will unite to invade the Land of Israel. The Sages tell us that Gog will come to attack us in three major wars; the first two are discussed in the two chapters of Yechezkel cited, and the last battle is in Zechariah.[299]

These battles are meant to be so terrifying that even the Sages Ula and Rabbah prayed to G-d that while they wished the Mashiach to come, they rather would not be alive to see his actual arrival since it would come with tremendous suffering and hardship.[300]

We have different interpretations as to who Gog and Magog actually are. It's also unclear which three wars the Sages are talking

---

296   *Midrash Tehillim* 22:9.
297   *Yechezkel,* chaps. 38–39.
298   *Zechariah* 14.
299   *Midrash Tehillim* 109.
300   *Sanhedrin* 98b.

about. Modern-day scholars suggest that the first two wars will not take place in the Land of Israel and are actually a reference to the First and Second World Wars. The third will thus be the Third World War that has not happened yet, which will be the final battle and will take place in Israel.

Rashi is of the opinion that Gog is the name of the king, and Magog is the name of the nation.[301]

The *Midrash Tanchumah* points out that the numerical value of the sum of the words Gog and Magog are seventy.[302] The number seventy represents the seventy nations of the world, so Gog and Magog is a reference to the entire world coming to attack Israel as one.

Some interpret this final war as not involving the Jewish people at all. According to Abarbanel, this final battle will be between Gog, who is Edom (the Christian nations), and Magog who is Yishmael (the Arab nations).[303] The battle will take place in the vicinity of Yerushalayim, and Israel will watch the events but may not actually be directly involved.

The Malbim writes that Magog represents both Christians and Muslims. They will all come together to Israel to capture the Land, but in the process, there will be fighting amongst themselves and many will die in the process of the battle.[304]

It is told about one of the great rabbinic leaders of the last generation, Rabbi Yaakov Yisrael Kanievsky, also known as the Steipler, that on Purim one year, around fifty years ago, he announced that we are very close to the coming of the Mashiach, and since we went through most of the birth pains of the Mashiach during World War Two with all of its dreadful suffering, this may qualify (aligned with Rashi's opinion above) as the battle of Gog and Magog.[305]

---

301   *Yechezkel* 38:2.
302   *Parashas Korach.*
303   Abarbanel, *Yechezkel* 32:17.
304   Malbim, *Yechezkel* 32:17.
305   *Orchos Rabbeinu*, vol. 1, pg. 287.

WHO ARE GOG AND MAGOG?

The exact identity of Gog and Magog is shrouded in mystery. Seemingly we won't be aware of who they are until they actually appear on the battlefield of world history. However, we do have some hints as to who they may actually be. According to Yechezkel, the location that Gog comes from is the "farthest north."[306] Josephus identifies the descendants of Magog as the Scythians, who before the Common Era branched out eastward and westward from the region north of the Black Sea.[307] The Talmud Yerushalmi seems to concur with this opinion and identifies Magog as coming from Gutya, or the Goths.[308] The Goths were a group of nomadic tribes who destroyed the Scythians and took over their land.

What's incredible about this identification is that the Goths were a Germanic people. The Targum Yonasan, written around 50 BCE, renders the name Magog as Germamia,[309] which the Midrash writes as Germaniah,[310] or Germany. This could explain the almost inexplicable way the Germans treated the Jewish people during the Second World War, which may be the second of the three battles Yechezkel is discussing.

A tradition from the Vilna Gaon, who lived in the eighteenth century, is mentioned in a book called *Chevlei Mashiach Bizmaneinu*; that when the Russian Navy passes through the Bosphorus, it will be time to put on your Shabbos clothes and prepare for the coming of the Mashiach.[311]

---

306   *Yechezkel* 38:15.

307   Josephus, *Antiquities* 1:6.

308   *Megillah* 3:9.

309   *Bereishis* 10:2.

310   *Bereishis Rabbah* 37:1.

311   According to Wikipedia, this is a natural strait and an internationally significant waterway located in northwestern Turkey that forms part of the continental boundary between Europe and Asia and separates Asian Turkey from European Turkey. It is the world's narrowest strait used for international navigation. The Bosphorus connects the Black Sea with the Sea of Marmara, and, by extension via the Dardanelles, the Aegean, and Mediterranean Seas.

In addition, Yechezkel refers to other nation-states that will join Gog's forces, "Persia, Cush, and Put."[312] We know that modern-day Persia is Iran. Cush lies to the south of Egypt between the southern Nile Valley and the Red Sea, which today is the eastern part of the Sudan, Ethiopia, and Eritrea. According to Josephus, Put is Libya.[313] It seems that much of the turmoil in the region will be at the hands of the children of Yishmael, who are the modern-day Islamic nations.

Even though we have many opinions as to who Gog and Magog actually are, in his commentary to the Bible, the late Chief Rabbi of the British Empire, Dr. J. H. Hertz, writes that "the identity of Gog is obscure, and he is probably to be understood as an apocalyptic figure, personifying the forces hostile to Israel, rather than a particular person."[314]

WHEN DOES THE FINAL BATTLE TAKE PLACE?

According to Yechezkel, the final war takes place when the Jews are living in Israel in peace. This implies that this battle takes place after Mashiach comes, as it says: "So said G-d, 'Surely on that day, when My people Israel dwells securely…when you come from your place in the outermost parts of the north, you and many people with you…a mighty army, and you advance against My people, like a cloud covering the earth.'"[315]

However, according to Zechariah the prophet, who also discusses the battle, he writes that after the battle G-d's Name will be one, implying that perhaps this battle takes place before Mashiach comes.[316]

The Rambam sides with the approach that the war of Gog and Magog will happen soon after the arrival of Mashiach.[317] He writes: "It seems from the simple meaning of the words of the prophets that in the beginning of the days of the Mashiach, there will be a war between Gog and

---

312   *Yechezkel* 38:5.

313   *Antiquities loc. cit.*

314   Rabbi Dr. J. H. Hertz, commentary on the Bible, pg. 979.

315   *Yechezkel* 38:14–16.

316   *Zechariah* 14:7–9.

317   Rambam, *Mishneh Torah, Melachim* 12:2.

Magog, and that before the war between Gog and Magog, a prophet will rise to straighten Israel out and to prepare their hearts, as it is written, 'Behold, I am sending to you Eliyahu HaNavi.'"[318]

WHY ARE THEY ATTACKING US?

When Yechezkel the Prophet describes this war, he speaks of it as an attack on the people who return from exile to Israel, living peacefully within their boundaries, following agricultural and commercial pursuits, and prospering in their Land. They are so prosperous that the other nations become jealous and attack to obtain spoils of war, including silver and gold.

According to the Maharal of Prague, the real reason for these attacks by the other nations is plain anti-Semitism and nothing more.[319] They have such a hatred of G-d's chosen people and their mission in the world that they attack us not for financial gain, but simply to destroy our nation because of who we are and what we represent.[320]

Ultimately, this is all part of G-d's plan to finally remove evil from the world and to bring a world of true peace into existence.

GOG AND MAGOG — THE BATTLE OF THE ROOF PEOPLE

We have a tradition that goes back to Rav Hai Gaon that the final victory over Gog and Magog will take place in Tishrei, which is the same month that Rosh Hashanah, Yom Kippur, and Succos occur.[321] Rabbi Samson Raphael Hirsch makes a very deep and profound connection between Succos and the war of Gog and Magog.[322] He points out that in the Hebrew word *Gog* we see the word *gag*, which means a roof.

> A roof symbolizes the self-made stability and safety people find though their own achievements.

---

318   *Malachi* 2:23.
319   Maharal, *Chiddushei Aggados*.
320   Actually they lose monetary resources by attacking us. Look at how many military and financial resources Hitler and the Nazis were willing to divert just to destroy Jews during the Holocaust when they could have used those resources to help their war effort.
321   Quoted in *Nimukei Yosef, Megillah*.
322   Rabbi Samson Raphael Hirsch, *Bamidbar* 29:13.

A roof symbolizes the self-made stability and safety people find though their own achievements. Such people see the roof and homes they own that they themselves have built as being their true source of protection, and not their faith in G-d.

The opposite are the *succah* dwellers. The *succah* is covered by a sparse and leaky roof made up of vegetation that has been disconnected from the ground. Every Succos we leave the comfort of our homes, and for seven days we live under the protection of an insufficient roof. By doing so, we place our entire faith in G-d as our Ultimate Protector.

THE GENERATION WITH A FACE OF A DOG

One of the expressions used to describe the generation before the Mashiach's arrival is found at the end of the Mishnah in *Sotah*: "The face of the generation will be like the face of a dog."[323] What is the meaning of this cryptic phrase? It must be more than just an insult to us who are alive at this incredible time!

One opinion is that this is a reference to the lack of shame of the people living before the Mashiach's arrival. Just like a dog acts in a brazen way, doing all of its deeds in the open in front of everyone, so too will the generation before the Mashiach's arrival behave in an open and unashamed way, performing acts normally kept for the private sphere in the most open and unashamed way.

Rabbi Yisrael Salanter gives the following incredible understanding of who exactly the "face of the generation" is referring to.[324] The face of the generation is a reference to its leaders. The people who lead are the people whose faces are seen by all and represent us in society. But why are the leaders referred to as the face of a dog? Well, if you've ever seen someone lead his dog, it should become quite apparent. When a person walks his dog, he allows his dog to run ahead of him. As an outsider, we may see the dog ahead of its master and think that the dog is leading and is therefore the master.

---

323   *Sotah*, end of chap. 9.
324   Quoted by Rabbi Elchanan Wasserman, *Ikvesa D'Meshicha*, pg. 19.

All this changes, however, when the true master makes a turn in the direction they were walking. As soon as the dog senses that his master is walking the other way, he turns his face backwards and makes a complete turn from the way he was going before.

So too, before the Mashiach comes, says Rabbi Yisrael Salanter, we will see leaders seeming to lead, but really they are like the dog walking ahead of the master. The masses of people they are meant to be leading are really deciding the direction society is going in. As soon as the whims of the masses go in a certain direction, the leaders of the generation turn their heads and double-back in the direction that the people are going.

This is therefore a sign that before the Mashiach, we won't have real leaders but a group of individuals who merely make decisions not based on any belief system, but on what they think the people they lead want them to do.

HOW LONG WILL THE WAR OF GOG AND MAGOG LAST?

Regarding the exact length of the battle of Gog and Magog, the Vilna Gaon and the Chafetz Chaim have different opinions as to how long this final war will last. The Vilna Gaon states that the final war of Gog and Magog will begin on Hoshana Rabbah before daybreak and will last three hours.[325] It was said in the name of the Chafetz Chaim that World War Three will be Gog and Magog, and it may last a total of twenty minutes![326]

The prophet Yoel uses an unusual turn of phrase when describing the final war: "I will set wonders in the heavens and on earth: blood and fire and pillars of smoke; the sun will turn to darkness and the moon to blood-red before the coming of the great and awesome Day of Hashem."[327] The phrase for "pillar of smoke" in Hebrew is *simras ashan*. This literally means a "palm-tree of smoke," which also can be understood as a mushroom cloud. This may be a reference to some form of nuclear war. This

---

325   Vilna Gaon, commentary to the *Mechilta*, *Shemos* 14:20.
326   Rabbi Yechezkel Levenstein, cited in *Ohr Yechezkel*.
327   *Yoel* 3:3–4.

fits in with the amount of time the war will last, according to the Vilna Gaon and the Chafetz Chaim above.

By the end of the war, many corpses will be strewn around the Land and will be left unburied. Eventually Gog will succumb in the battle and be killed. Since the Land of Israel is holy land, and the sight of a corpse unburied would be disrespectful to its holiness, the Jewish people will actually begin burying the corpses.

Do all these negative prophecies of impending war actually *have* to happen? If the prophets speak of war and suffering, isn't there something we can do to avert the decree?

HAVE FAITH IN G-D

The Seforno explains:

> *The prophet Yoel promises that all those who refer to G-d in their everyday conversation will survive the wars preceding the coming of the Mashiach.[328] Their mentioning of G-d is considered proof of their believing in Him. The difference of the Jewish people lies in the fact that they do not turn to soothsayers, and all kinds of charlatans, astrologers, or palm readers to divine the future.*

> *If they want to know something about the future, they turn to G-d directly or to a prophet, or they are content to let G-d do what He considers to be right. We see from Yeshayah,[329] as well as from Zechariah,[330] that when the time comes, the Jewish people, who have been steadfast in their loyalty to G-d, will share in the ultimate salvation. The Jews at that time will finally be recognized as deserving a position of leadership amongst mankind.[331]*

---

328 *Yoel* 3:5.
329 *Yeshayah* 61:6.
330 *Zechariah* 8:23.
331 *Bereishis* 49:26.

NEGATIVE PROPHECIES DON'T NEED TO HAPPEN — BUT GOOD ONES DO

Although the war and its aftermath are described in the prophets and many commentaries, none of this *needs* to happen. Negative decrees and prophecies can be averted, but positive prophecies must come true. The Rambam makes this point when he says:

> *As to calamities predicted by a prophet, if for example he foretells the death of a certain individual or declares that in a particular year there will be famine or war and so forth, the non-fulfillment of his forecast does not disprove his prophetic character.*
>
> *We are not to say, "See, he spoke and his prediction has not come to pass." For G-d is patient and abounding in kindness and forgiving of evil. It may also be that those who were threatened repented and were therefore forgiven, as happened to the men of Nineveh… But if the prophet, in the name of G-d, assures good fortune, declaring that a particular event would come to pass, and the benefit promised has not been realized, he is unquestionably a false prophet, for no blessing decreed by the Almighty, even if promised conditionally, is ever revoked… Hence we learn that only when he predicts good fortune can the prophet be tested.*[332]

So a prophet can be given a message outlining the possible consequences if the people do not follow the path of goodness. If the people do make a turnaround and change their ways, the evil decree against them can be averted.

The classic case can be found in *Sefer Yonah*. Yonah is commanded by G-d to warn the people of Nineveh that their wickedness is about to bring disaster on them. Yonah attempts to flee, but fails — the famous story of the sea, the storm, and the great fish. Eventually he goes to

---

332   Rambam, *Mishneh Torah, Yesodei HaTorah* 10:4.

Nineveh and utters the words G-d has commanded him to say — "Forty more days and Nineveh will be destroyed" — the people repent, and the city is spared. Yonah, however, is deeply dissatisfied: "But Yonah was greatly displeased and became angry. He prayed to the Lord, 'O Lord, is this not what I said when I was still at home? That is why I was so quick to flee to Tarshish. I knew that you are a gracious and compassionate G-d, slow to anger and abounding in love, a G-d who relents from sending calamity. Now, O Lord, take away my life, for it is better for me to die than to live.'"[333]

Why was Yonah so upset? He didn't realize that G-d does not wish to harm anybody, and Yonah's mission was to help the people of Nineveh repent, not to inform them that G-d was about to destroy them. So when they heard of the impending disaster, they changed their ways, and they were spared.

Yonah was wrong to be displeased. G-d asks Yonah a rhetorical question with which the book concludes: "Should I not be concerned about that great city?" In essence, should I not be merciful? Should I not forgive?

So too, even though the prophets have spoken about possible calamities at the End of Days, none of them need occur if we change our actions and begin to care for each other the way the Torah commands us to.

AMALEK — THE UPROOTING OF EVIL

The battle of Gog and Magog will be the last war known to mankind. The Rambam states that the main difference between the world before and after the Mashiach comes is that the Jewish people will no longer be a persecuted nation. In fact, all armies will cease to exist, and all disputes between nation-states will come to an end.

> The Jewish people will no longer be a persecuted nation.

However, that is after the Mashiach comes. Before the Mashiach can truly bring peace to the earth, evil must be eradicated. The final battle

---

333 *Yonah* 4:1–3.

between good and evil will end with the eradication of the nation of Amalek. According to the *Akeidas Yitzchak*, this is necessary because "only after the formal defeat of the kingdom of Amalek could the Mashiach begin his career on earth. After all the wrangling between the forces of those against G-d and Israel will have ended, Israel and its Messianic king will emerge as mightier than the forces against them."[334]

MASHIACH BEN YOSEF

The Mashiach we have been speaking about until now is the king who is a direct descendant of David HaMelech from the tribe of Yehudah. He is therefore known as Mashiach ben David, Mashiach the son of David. However, the Talmud quotes the prophet Zechariah and writes about another Mashiach who will precede the Mashiach ben David, and will come from the tribe of Ephraim, the son of Yosef.[335] He is therefore known as Mashiach ben Yosef, Mashiach the son of Joseph.[336] These two individuals are really two stages of one process.

Very little is known about the exact nature of this first Mashiach, even though much is written in Kabbalistic works about him. We do know however that the primary function of Mashiach ben Yosef is of a political and military nature. The *Pirkei Mashiach* describes Mashiach ben Yosef in the following way: "Mashiach ben Yosef will take them up to Yerushalayim, build the Temple, and bring sacrifices, whereupon a fire will come down from heaven and consume their sacrifices."[337] This will occur forty years before the Mashiach ben David will reveal himself. Mashiach ben Yosef will be a representative of Mashiach ben David and will smooth the path for him by being active in gathering the Jews to Israel and in cleansing the people from their sins.

He will also be involved in waging wars. The main battle will be against the forces of Edom, the Christian leaders, and they will be headed by

---

334   *Akeidas Yitzchak* 82:82.
335   *Zechariah* 12:10.
336   *Succah* 52a.
337   *Pirkei Mashiach, Beis HaMedresh* part 3.

someone referred to in the literature as Armilus. The prophet Ovadiah makes a reference to this battle when he says, "The House of Yaakov will be fire, the House of Yosef a flame, and the House of Eisav for straw, and they will ignite them and devour them."[338]

So although Israel will be victorious during this battle, still Mashiach ben Yosef will be killed in it. Zechariah the Prophet refers to this when he says, "They will look towards Me because of those whom they have stabbed; they will mourn over him as one mourns over an only child, and be embittered over him like the embitterment over a deceased firstborn."[339] These words, says the Talmud, are a reference to the death of Mashiach ben Yosef who will be greatly mourned and eulogized.[340] Some, however, believe that his death is not certain and that the decree for him to die was nullified.[341]

Rav Hai Gaon gives a remarkable description of Mashiach ben Yosef of how his support will grow. He will begin in the Galilee region in the north of Israel where he will gather support for his mission by assembling followers. He will then make his way down south to Yerushalayim and will announce his mission to the world. When word of this goes out — that Yerushalayim is to be captured — the other nations will come and try to defeat this new king of Israel.[342]

Having said all this, Rav Sa'adiah Gaon writes that if we merit the coming of the Mashiach though our good deeds and repentance, we won't even need the Mashiach ben Yosef.[343] Accordingly, Mashiach ben Yosef will only come if we don't merit the Mashiach's arrival at the time of the Redemption. In that less-miraculous scenario, we will need the Mashiach ben Yosef to pave the way for the ultimate Mashiach, as we explained above.

---

338   *Ovadiah* 1:18.
339   *Zechariah* 12:10.
340   *Succah* 52a.
341   Ramchal, *Kinas Hashem Tzevaos* (Bnei Brak 1980).
342   Rav Hai Gaon, *Al Inyan HaYeshua.*
343   Rav Sa'adiah Gaon, *Emunos VeDei'os* 8.

Finally, according to Rabbi Avraham Yitzchak Kook, Mashiach ben Yosef isn't even a single person but is actually a time.[344] So the entire return to the Land of Israel by the Jewish people and the subsequent wars we faced in the latter part of the twentieth century could already be the fulfillment of the Mashiach ben Yosef and his mission.

---

344   Rabbi Avraham Yitzchak HaKohen Kook, *Orot* 160.

Chapter Eighteen

PURIM AND THE MASHIACH — WHAT'S THE CONNECTION?

IT WOULD BE difficult for us to fully understand the process of the Mashiach's arrival without an example. Fortunately, we have the perfect example from Jewish history that allows us to not only understand, but even to experience the Mashiach's arrival. That example is the Purim story.

After the destruction of the First Temple in Yerushalayim by the Babylonians, the Jews were exiled to Babylonia and other countries around the world. After the Babylonians came the Persian exile, and the Jews found themselves in Persia under the control of a cruel tyrant, Achashverosh, and his second-in-command, the evil Haman. Fortunately, the Jewish people were saved by Esther and Mordechai, who (with G-d's help) were able to formulate a plan to save the Jews from Haman's nefarious plan.

What is it about the Purim story that can reveal something to us about the Mashiach's arrival? Let's examine the Purim story to see what it can reveal about the Mashiach and the way he may arrive.

THE PURIM PARADIGM AND THE MASHIACH

On the surface, the Purim story seems like a string of coincidences: Achashverosh decides to kill his wife Vashti, and then from all the women in his vast kingdom he chooses Esther to replace her. Mordechai happens to overhear two of Achashverosh's servants, Bigsan and Seresh, planning to assassinate the king. Mordechai then tells Esther, who informs Achashverosh of the plot to kill him. Achashverosh then writes down his desire to reward Mordechai, which he ends up doing at just the right moment, which then leads to the downfall of Haman and brings an end to the decree that Haman had made with Achashverosh to destroy the Jewish people.

Achashverosh permits Mordechai and Esther to save the Jewish people worldwide, and what would have been a day of great pain and sorrow ends up becoming the greatest salvation the Jewish people had ever experienced since walking free from tyrannical Pharaoh when they left Egypt with Moshe Rabbeinu many years before. The Purim story, say the commentaries, has within it the secret of the entire future of the Mashiach.

> The Purim story has within it the secret of the entire future of the Mashiach.

PURIM, PART TWO

When we look at the Purim story, we can't see G-d operating the story at all. Just like the name of the heroine of the Purim story indicates — Esther, which in Hebrew means "hidden" — G-d is completely hidden in the story. Actually, *Megillas Esther*, which retells the story of Purim, is the only book in all of the Scriptures where G-d's Name is never actually mentioned. This is because G-d hides Himself in the nature of the events. We are expected to see G-d orchestrating the events as we read the story and attempt to see His guiding Hand as the different parts of the story reveal themselves.

Before the Mashiach comes, it will be very hard for us to "see" G-d operating in the pre-Messianic turmoil. It will appear that G-d has totally removed Himself from the stage of history and is allowing things to just happen in a random and unplanned fashion. This will lead many among the Jewish people to ask, "Is G-d really with us, or are we all alone?" Well, just like G-d orchestrated the Purim story, so too is He in full control of the events that lead up to the Final Redemption and the Mashiach.

The Chafetz Chaim takes the connection between the Purim story and the pre-Messianic era even further.[345] He writes that at the time of the Purim story the evil Haman had decreed death upon every Jew throughout the entire world. Since Achashverosh ruled over 127 provinces around the world, you could assume that every Jew was threatened with annihilation. The decree of Haman was signed, sealed, and even delivered to all those provinces, permitting anyone living near any Jews to kill them and take all their possessions without any legal recourse from the ruler Achashverosh. Who wouldn't be tempted to attack and kill a helpless Jew at that time and in turn become very wealthy?

Together with the decree came a date chosen by Haman himself to wipe out the Jews: man, woman and child — the thirteenth day of the Jewish month of Adar. The entire machinery was now in place for the complete annihilation of the Jews worldwide. Who, asks the Chafetz Chaim, would ever believe that the Jews could do anything to reverse that decree? Not only that, but even the hero of the story, Mordechai, was destined to be killed eleven months earlier. Haman requested of Achashverosh special permission to kill the Jewish people, because of his anger at Mordechai who had refused to bow down to him. Achasheverosh gave Haman permission to do this by giving Haman his ring. Haman, together with his ten sons, built an enormous gallows to publicly hang Mordechai for all to see.

Eventually, at risk to her own life, and if unsuccessful, potentially all the Jewish people, the great prophetess Esther was able to plead with Achashverosh and to accuse Haman of being the true threat to the Jewish people and to Achashverosh and his kingdom. After Haman was caught by Achashverosh in a very compromising position with Esther (when in reality he was merely pleading at her feet for forgiveness) Haman was given a decree of death. The gallows that were built by Haman to hang Mordechai were now used to hang Haman. Later, the same gallows was used to hang Haman's ten sons as well.

---

345   Chafetz Chaim, *Shem Olam* 14.

Today we see the Jewish people are just as spread out as they were in the days of Mordechai and Esther. This, says the Chafetz Chaim, should not be a source of concern, although it may seem that we are more vulnerable as a nation because of it. On the contrary, this is a sign that the Final Redemption is at hand and G-d is about to lift us up from the lowest places to the heights of greatness. Since the Jewish people are dispersed throughout the world, the inhabitants of the world will see the Jews leave their countries and cities and be fully aware of the redemptive process as it happens.

THE SPEEDY REDEMPTION

Another key characteristic of the redemption of Purim was the incredible speed with which things turned around. The actual story took nearly twenty years to unfold. However, once the redemption process began, we went from near annihilation to complete redemption in an instant. This idea is found in a famous dictum: "*Yeshuas Hashem keheref ayin* — G-d's redemption can occur in the blink of an eye."[346]

> G-d's redemption can occur in the blink of an eye.

Let's revisit the story once again to see this point in action. The entire Jewish people were convinced they were about to be wiped out. They had no army or any military training. Any influence they may have had in the government was about to be wiped out with them. This was the end for them, and there was no way out. Some say that the Jewish people were not aware that Esther, who was married to Achashverosh, was even Jewish, and even if they were aware she was Jewish, they didn't believe she had any ability to save them. From that low point of no way out, they were miraculously saved and given the chance to return to Israel to begin again and even rebuild the Second Temple in Yerushalayim. No one saw this coming. Even Esther did not believe she would survive informing Achashverosh of her background, when she said, "If I die, then I die."

---

346   *Pesikta Zutra, Esther* 4:17.

From this point, everything, as the Megillah states, *nehafachu*, turned around. Our enemies were dispatched, Mordechai was reinstated to honor and glory, and Esther remained queen. All this happened in an instant.

The same formula will occur right before the Mashiach reveals himself. Life for the Jewish people will seem absolutely lost. We will turn to G-d and say, "Where will we find Redemption?" Just when we are convinced all is lost and nothing worse can happen, just then the Redemption will occur, and when it does, it will be another *nehafachu*, a complete and utter reversal of events that will usher in the Final Redemption. Whether the Redemption will follow the natural order of events like the Purim story, or be a miraculous one like the Pesach events, is totally up to us.

MEGILLAS ESTHER — THE ETERNAL BOOK

The Rambam makes the following astonishing statement about the nature of the Jewish Scriptures once the Mashiach arrives: "All the books of the Prophets and all the Holy Writings will be nullified in the Messianic era, with the exception of *Megillas Esther*. It will continue to exist, as will the Five Books of the Torah and the halachos of the Oral Law, which will never be nullified."[347]

This is hinted at in *Megillas Esther* where it says, "And these days of Purim will not pass from among the Jews, nor will their remembrance cease from their seed."[348] This means that when the Mashiach comes, we will forget all the difficulties endured by our people throughout Jewish history. The memory of them will be forgotten. The prophet Yeshayah made reference to this when he said, "For the former difficulties will be forgotten and for they will be hidden from My eye."[349] But the celebration of the days of Purim will not be nullified or forgotten. This is because the redemptive quality of Purim will be so great and

---

347 Rambam, *Mishneh Torah*, *Megilah U'Chanukah* 2:18.
348 *Esther* 9:28.
349 *Yeshayah* 65:16.

meaningful for the Messianic era — when we won't need the words of the prophets anymore — because the redemption of which they spoke will have happened with the arrival of the Mashiach. *Megillas Esther*, however, will always be with us, as its significance far surpasses the events that happened in Persia all those years ago.

Chapter Nineteen

ELIYAHU HANAVI — NOT JUST A PASSOVER SEDER GUEST

ONE OF THE key characters in the unfolding of the Messianic drama is Eliyahu HaNavi. Eliyahu is the prophet who will herald the arrival of the Mashiach. Together with the Mashiach he will bring an enduring peace to all the inhabitants of the world.

We first meet Eliyahu in the Book of Kings, where he is referred to as *Eliyahu HaTishbi*, Eliyahu the Tishbite, which Rashi explains to mean that he came from a city called Toshav. Some say that Tishbi is related to the word *teshuvah*, repentance, because Eliyahu had the power to bring people back to G-d and repent through his spoken word. The vision of him in Scriptures is as a prophet who recognized his mission as that of someone who could not remain silent when people spoke or acted in ways that disparaged the word of G-d.

Let's consider a few stories about Eliyahu in order to better understand who he was and what role he will play in the Future Redemption.

ELIYAHU RESUSCITATES A YOUNG BOY

The Book of Kings tells us that G-d sent Eliyahu to Tsarfasah, where a poor widow would provide him with food and water. [350] When Eliyahu

---

350 *Melachim I* 17:17–24.

asked her for some bread, she responded that all she had in the house was a handful of flour and a little bit of oil, just enough for her and her son to survive on. Eliyahu told her not to despair, a miracle occurred, and she had enough food for herself and her household for a year.

Soon after this, her son became deathly ill, and according to many commentators,[351] the boy actually died. Eliyahu took the boy and brought him to the upper story where he was staying and laid him on his bed. He prayed to G-d and stretched himself out over the boy three times. The boy then came back to life.

Since this woman had been so kind to him, Eliyahu felt obliged to reciprocate the many favors she had done for him, and in this case it paid off as the boy was revived. The young boy grew up to be none other than Yonah the Prophet, a great person in his own right.

THE CHALLENGE OF ELIYAHU AT MOUNT CARMEL

A famous story involving Eliyahu HaNavi was the episode at Mount Carmel. Worship of the idol Baal had become rampant throughout the Northern Kingdom in Israel. Frustrated with the popularity of this form of idol worship and the general decline in the allegiance to the G-d of Israel, Eliyahu knew he had to take a stand.

He approached all the people and said, "How long will you dance between two opinions? If Hashem is the G-d go after Him! And if Baal, go after it!"[352] Eliyahu then issued a challenge, "I alone have remained as a prophet of G-d, and the prophets of Baal are four hundred and fifty men. Let us be given two bulls. Let them choose one bull for themselves, cut it, and put it on the wood, and I will prepare the other bull and put it on the wood. You call out to your gods and I will call out in the name of Hashem. Whichever responds with fire, He is the true G-d." The challenge was accepted.

The followers of Baal set up their sacrifice but nothing happened, "They called out from morning to noon saying, 'O Baal answer us.' But

---

351   See Rashi and Metsudas Tzion, *Melachim I* 17:17. The Radak cites an opinion that he was deathly ill and so near death that his breath and pulse could hardly be detected.
352   *Melachim I* 18:21–24.

there was neither sound nor response...Eliyahu ridiculed them and said, 'Cry out in a loud voice, for he is a god.' They called out in a loud voice and cut themselves with swords and spears, but there was neither sound nor response nor listener."

When the time came for Eliyahu to have his offering accepted, not only did he place the bull on the wood, but he even soaked the wood and sacrifice with jugs of water. He then prayed to the G-d of Avraham, Yitzchak, and Yaakov, and asked G-d to answer him, then "A fire of G-d descended and consumed the sacrifice and the wood, the stones, and the earth."[353]

ELIYAHU HANAVI ASCENDS TO HEAVEN

The final prophet Malachi, in his final prophecy, describes Eliyahu's arrival in the following way, "Behold I send you Eliyahu HaNavi before the coming of the great and awesome day of Hashem."[354] His return will actually constitute the very first person to be resurrected from the dead. This will be because when Eliyahu ascended to heaven in a whirlwind, a fiery chariot and fiery horses appeared. He was taken into this chariot where his body and his clothes were consumed by fire, and his soul returned to its maker.[355] Before the Mashiach comes, G-d will create a body in the likeness of Eliyahu's original one and place his soul in that body and send him to bring the Jewish people back to G-d. Some say Eliyahu will be the first to be resurrected from the dead. Reish Lakish says that Eliyahu never actually died, meaning that his soul never actually departed from his body.[356]

The Midrash informs us of the role Eliyahu HaNavi will have before the coming of the Mashiach.[357] Quoting this statement from Zechariah the Prophet:

"Sing and be glad, O daughter of Zion! For behold I am coming and I will dwell in your midst — the word of Hashem."[358]

---

353   Ibid. 18:30–35.
354   *Malachi* 3:23.
355   *Melachim II* 2:1–11.
356   *Moed Katan* 26a.
357   *Pesikta Rabasi* 35.
358   *Zechariah* 2:14.

The Midrash tells us when this statement of the prophet will occur:

When will this occur? At the time when the Holy One, Blessed Be He, will redeem Israel. Three days before the coming of the Mashiach, Eliyahu will arrive and stand upon the mountains of Israel, and he will cry and lament over them saying, "Mountains of the Land of Israel, until when will you remain standing in ruin, desolation, and destruction?" His voice will be heard from one end of the world to the other. Afterward he will say to them, "Peace has come to the world," as is written, "Behold on the mountains the feet of the herald proclaiming peace!"[359] When the wicked will hear this, they will rejoice and say to each other, "Peace has come to us."

On the second day Eliyahu will come and stand on the mountains of Israel and say, "Goodness has come to the world," as is written, "Heralding good tidings."[360] On the third day he will come and say, "Salvation has come to the world," as is written, "Proclaiming salvation."

So Malachi the Prophet was informing us that the herald of the final Mashiach will be none other than the great prophet Eliyahu himself. The fact that the very last communication from G-d to His people invoked the name of Eliyahu HaNavi should serve as a source of great hope and inspiration for us all. G-d Himself was comforting us that although the Temple would be destroyed, and prophecy would be lost from our people for over two thousand years, we would still have the words of Malachi with us reminding us that the Final Redemption would eventually be at hand!

---

359   *Nachum* 2:1.
360   *Yeshayah* 52:7.

ELIYAHU'S PLEDGE TO YAAKOV

The Midrash tells us the amazing connection between Yaakov and Eliyahu HaNavi.[361] The Torah in *Vayikra* says, "I will remember my covenant with Yaakov."[362]

The Midrash says, "The word Eliyahu is always spelled fully with a *vav* except for five instances. Yaakov is always spelled missing a *vav* except for five instances. This is to teach you that Eliyahu will come to redeem the offspring of Yaakov, as it says, "Behold I send you Eliya(hu) HaNavi..."[363]

In Hebrew, Eliyahu's name can be written with or without the letter *vav*. In this verse from Malachi quoted above, and in another four places, the name is written lacking the letter *vav*.[364] Rashi notes that there are also five places in Scripture where the name Yaakov is spelled differently and given an extra *vav*. He explains that Yaakov took the *vav* from Eliyahu's name as a security that Eliyahu will come and herald the redemption of the Jewish people.[365]

The Maharal of Prague in *Gur Aryeh* clarifies that we learn from this Midrash that Eliyahu's task to herald the Redemption is integral to his very existence. Until Eliyahu does so, we are to regard him as being incomplete. However, once that task is accomplished, the *vav* will be returned to his name, which will symbolize that the man and his mission have been fulfilled.

The Maharal then asks three questions:

> Yaakov grasped the hand of Eliyahu, making him promise that he would one day rescue his children from exile.

- Why was Yaakov the one who took this pledge and not anybody else?
- Why was the letter *vav* taken from his name rather than any other letter?
- And why was the letter *vav* taken five times?

---

361 *Midrash Chaseiros VeYaseiros*, found in *Otzar Midrashim*, pg. 197.
362 *Vayikra* 26:42.
363 *Malachi* 3:23.
364 *Melachim II* 1:3, 4, 8, 12.
365 *Vayikra* 26:42.

He answers that Yaakov, unlike Avraham and Yitzchak who each had a son not destined to be redeemed by the Mashiach, would have all of his children redeemed by the Mashiach. The letter *vav* looks like a finger, and therefore five *vavs* represent a hand. Agreements and pledges are signified by a handshake. So, in essence, it was as if Yaakov grasped the hand of Eliyahu, making him promise that he would one day rescue his children from exile.

Finally, just as Eliyahu's name is deemed incomplete until the End of Days, so too true peace will not be full until his arrival and the Final Redemption.

His arrival will be three days before the Mashiach reveals himself,[366] but he will not appear right before Shabbos or a Jewish festival so as not to disrupt preparations for these holy days. One day before he announces the coming of the Mashiach, Eliyahu will inform the other nations of the world that the coming of the Mashiach is imminent and he will prepare them for this moment.

THE CUP OF ELIYAHU HANAVI

Placing a fifth cup of wine on the Passover Seder table (that we don't drink) is a widespread custom throughout the Jewish world. This cup is called the Cup of Eliyahu. A number of reasons are given for this custom of pouring a fifth cup and placing it on the Passover table. One is to connect it to the final Messianic Redemption at the End of Days. Let's see how.

The Midrash states that on Seder night, Eliyahu together with Mashiach will make their long-awaited appearance:[367]

> *Why is it written that the night of Passover is Leil Shimurim, a night of protection?[368] For on it He did great things for the righteous, just as He did for Israel in Egypt. On it he saved*

---

366   *Eruvin* 43a–b.
367   *Shemos Rabbah* 18:12.
368   *Shemos* 12:42.

Chizkiyahu, and on it He saved Chananiah and his friends, and on it He saved Daniel from the lions' den, and on it, Mashiach and Eliyahu will be exalted. For it is written, "The Watchman said, 'Morning is coming, but also night.'"[369]

This Midrash fits in with the opinion of Rav Yehoshua in the Talmud: "In the month of Nissan they were redeemed, and in the month of Nissan they are destined to be redeemed."[370] The miraculous night following the fourteenth of Nissan ushered in the redemption of the Jewish people from Egypt and that date and time would prove to remain as a time of miraculous redemption until the End of Days.

So the Cup of Eliyahu is placed on the Seder table to remind us of the redemptive quality of that night, not merely as a remembrance of the redemption of the Jewish people thousands of years ago from the hand of Egyptians. We place the Cup of Eliyahu in anticipation of the Mashiach's arrival that could occur that very night, and the cup is filled to the brim ready to be blessed over should the Mashiach arrive at that very moment.

POUR THE CUP AND OPEN THE DOOR

Rabbi Moshe Isserlis, also known at the Rama, adds to this another connected custom to open the front door during the Pesach Seder, "And the door is opened to remind us that it is a night of protection, and in the merit of that faith, Mashiach will come and he will pour his wrath upon those who oppose Hashem."[371]

The *Mishnah Berurah* explains, "It is customary in these lands to pour one cup more than the number of those participating in the meal and it is called the Cup of Eliyahu. We do this to indicate that we believe just as G-d redeemed us from Egypt, He will once again redeem us and will send Eliyahu to bring us that message."[372]

---

369   *Yeshayah* 21:12.
370   *Rosh Hashanah* 11a.
371   *Shulchan Aruch, Orach Chaim* 470:1.
372   *Mishnah Berurah* 480:10.

So as we sit at our Seder tables remembering the incredible deliverance of our forefathers and foremothers from Egyptian slavery all those years ago, we realize that the same G-d who redeemed us from that exile is waiting and anticipating the Redemption from this present exile as well.

THE FIFTH CUP

The Final Redemption of Mashiach also has an element of the number five related to it. We see this represented in the Pesach Seder. During the Seder we drink four cups of wine. Each one of these four cups comes to represent the four expressions the Torah uses to explain the four different parts of the redemption process. In the Messianic era, the Jewish people will be gathered from the four corners of the earth to the Land of Israel. The Land of Israel is represented here by the fifth dot on one face of the dice, as was mentioned above. It's the middle point and all points lead to that place.

At the Pesach Seder, therefore, we connect the two great redemptions of the Jewish people. The first happened over three thousand years ago in the Jewish year 2448 when the Jewish people left Egypt; that is the first part of the Pesach Seder. The latter part of the Pesach Seder, however, is really pointing us to the second great redemption of the Jewish people, which will occur in the times of the Mashiach who will be preceded by Eliyahu. This idea is represented by the fifth cup, which is left untouched on the Seder table, but will one day be drunk when the Mashiach finally arrives.

Chapter Twenty

CHILDREN RETURN THEIR PARENTS TO G-D

HISTORICALLY, IT HAS always been the way for parents to teach their children Torah and to guide them on the path to righteousness. However, Malachi's prophecy concludes with the words describing Eliyahu's mission: "And he will turn the hearts of the fathers back through the children, and the hearts of the children back through their fathers."[373]

Malachi's words seem a little counterintuitive. Instead of parents teaching their children Torah and thereby bringing their children to G-d, it seems like things will be the other way round — children teaching their parents! Rashi explains this to mean that Eliyahu will appear and return the hearts of the fathers to G-d through their children. So before the Mashiach comes, a process will begin of children teaching their parents about Torah and mitzvos instead of parents teaching their children, which was always the way among the Jewish people.

We can see clear evidence of the words of the prophet happening today. For the first time in many years, Torah is being embraced by the younger generation, and parents are being inspired by their children's commitment to Torah, Israel, and Jewish life, which in many cases they themselves never grew up with themselves.

---

373   *Malachi* 3:24.

The last Mishnah in *Eduyos* cites four opinions as to the exact nature of the mandate Eliyahu will have at the time of the Redemption.[374] Rav Yehoshua and Rav Yehudah say that Eliyahu's role will be to clarify the genealogical fitness of certain families. They disagree only in regard to the extent of that clarification. Rav Shimon says that Eliyahu will resolve disputes in the Torah. The Sages say that Eliyahu's task is to make peace in the world. Some interpret this to mean between nations in the world, others however say that Eliyahu will specifically bring peace between parents and their children.

How are these roles indicated in the words of Malachi quoted above? According to Rav Yehoshua and Rav Yehudah, the fathers will prevent their sons from inadvertently marrying women of questionable Jewish origin and sons will honor their fathers by heeding their requests and doing so intentionally. According to Rav Shimon, fathers and sons refer to teachers and their students. Eliyahu will resolve any and all disputes between them regarding how to interpret the Torah.

SOCIETY FINALLY COMES TOGETHER

According to the Sages, "fathers" is a reference to those who rule and control others, and "sons" is a reference to those under their control. When you have two classes in society, the ruling class and those under their control, much strife can occur between them. Many times the rulers will use their power to treat the disadvantaged unfairly, but also sometimes the downtrodden will also fail to recognize the compassion of their benefactors. With the arrival of Eliyahu, the fathers, i.e., the ruling class, will find themselves full of empathy for their sons, i.e., the lower class, and the hearts of the sons will swell with appreciation for the kindness of their fathers.

With these two parts of society now coming together as one, and both their hearts connecting to each other, society will be primed and ready to recognize the unity of G-d.

---

374   *Eduyos* 8:7.

The Rambam cites the opinion of the Sages in the Mishnah declaring it to be the decisive one:

> *He (Eliyahu) will not come to make the impure pure or to purify the impure. Nor will he come to disqualify those who have a status of being fit, nor to declare fit those believed to be disqualified. Rather, to establish peace in the world, as is written, "And he will turn back to G-d the hearts of fathers with their sons."*[375]

We are not precisely sure how Eliyahu will accomplish this epic feat of bringing peace upon the earth. Will it be miraculous or supernatural events that bring this era of peace upon earth, or will the course of events come through more natural means in the guise of people and governments coming together? Only time will tell. As the Rambam himself says in his concluding remarks:

> *And all these matters and their like, no man will know precisely how they will be, until they occur… Regardless, the order and details of these events are not fundamentals of our faith…they should not be considered essential, for they do not bring about fear of G-d nor love of G-d. Nor should one make calculations as to when will be the End of Days. The Sages said, "May the spirit of those who attempt to calculate the end suffer agony." Rather, one should wait and believe in the general principle of the matter, as we have explained.*

JEWS LOSING THEIR FAITH BEFORE THE MASHIACH COMES

Paradoxically, while many are coming back, one of the phenomena that will precede the Messianic age will be the loss of faith by many Jewish people of Jewish traditions and values. Stated in stronger terms, many Jews in the generation before the Mashiach comes will

---

375   Rambam, *Mishneh Torah, Melachim* 12:2.

begin to lose interest in being Jewish. A possible reason for this will be the incredible acceleration of modern technology that will create a huge chasm between the world parents live in and where their children live in. This generational divide will make communication between children and their parents extremely challenging.

Because of this distancing of the generations, children will have much less respect for their parents and will talk and act with great chutzpah to their elders. Much of this chutzpah will stem from the younger generations knowing much more than their elders about all areas of life, much of which they garner from social media and technology. Many children ask themselves how they are expected to respect a parent who knows so much less than them, and has such a narrow view of the world and isn't in touch with this ever-changing reality called life. Parents and children are literally living in different worlds.

In the words of the Mishnah: "Before the Mashiach comes: chutzpah will increase…truth will be absent, young people will blanch (embarrass) the faces of the elders, elders will rise in honor of the young people, a son will deride his father, a daughter will stand up against her mother and a daughter-in-law against her mother-in-law, the enemies of man will be members in his own household."[376]

One of the main victims of this distancing of the generations will be the amount of young people who feel no connection to their religion. The transmission of Judaism has always been from parent to child. Children have historically felt a connection to their Judaism and their Jewish identity primarily via their parents. If the connection between parent and child is eroded, one of the casualties will be the amount young people will be willing to identify with their parents' and grandparents' faith.

The Mishnah goes on to say: "The government will turn to heresy and become G-dless, and there will be no admonishment for sins, since all are sinners. Learning academies will become places of great immorality."

---

376 *Sotah*, end of chap. 9.

So much will this toxic environment affect the world that even the most pious among our people will be totally denigrated. The state of affairs will seem so bleak that the Mishnah seems to resign itself to the spiritual catastrophe that the world will be enduring at the End of Days. The Mishnah finally concludes with the desperate words after all these predictions: "Before the Mashiach comes, upon whom can we rely on? Only on our Father in Heaven."

JEWS RETURNING TO THEIR FAITH

As we've seen, even with atheism consuming the world, and the detachment of many Jews from their Jewish heritage, still many Jews will stubbornly hold on, while many others will return to the faith of their forefathers after many generations of alienation.

At the end of the Torah, Moshe Rabbeinu makes a reference to Jews at the End of Days returning to their heritage. It says: "It will be when all these things come upon you — the blessing and the curse that I have presented before you — then you will take it to your heart among all the nations where Hashem your G-d has dispersed you. And you will return to Hashem your G-d, and listen to His voice, according to everything I command you today, you and your children, with all your heart and all your soul."[377]

ATHEISM SWEEPING THE WORLD

As societies progress, the apparent need to rely on G-d and seek a relationship with Him will decline. A wave of atheism will sweep the world. Also, as science discovers more and begins to unravel the mysteries of the universe, people will be less inclined to admit they have a belief in G-d, even if they do, for fear of looking like a fool, as the Mishnah informed us, "Those who fear sin will be utterly despised."[378] It is because of this that many people will leave the fold of Judaism completely. This could also partly explain the high level of intermarriage we have seen steadily increase over the past few decades.

---

377 *Devarim* 30:1–2.
378 *Sotah* 9.

Although the Jewish people have characteristically been known as a very united group without too many divisions, this will not remain true for the generation before the Mashiach comes. The Jewish people will split into various groups, each laying claim to the truth. This will make it virtually impossible to discern true Judaism from the false ones. Yeshayah HaNavi predicted this when he said, "Truth will fail."[379]

JEWS FORSAKING JUDAISM

The Rambam discusses the words of the prophet Daniel when describing the End of Days, where he says, "Many shall purify themselves, and make themselves white, and be refined; but the wicked shall do wickedly; and none of the wicked shall understand; but they who are wise shall understand."[380]

On these words, the Rambam says:

> *We have a Divine prophecy from Daniel, where he foretold that as a result of the long stay in exile and the continuous persecutions, many would forsake our Jewish faith as doubt entered their minds and made them go astray. The primary reason for this breakdown is that they witnessed our weakness in contrast to our oppressors and their mastery over us. Others would not be plagued by doubts, their belief to the G-d of Israel and their faith would remain firm and unshaken.[381]*

According to the Rambam, Daniel is warning us that our lengthy stay in exile and seeing the apparent success of our host nations will break down our relationship with G-d and our Jewish faith. Some, however, will become purified as a result of their steadfast trust in G-d during this great trial.

The coming of the Mashiach will act as a transition from *Olam Hazeh*, the Present World, to *Olam Haba*, the Next World. Let's examine what life in *Olam Haba* will actually be like.

---

379   *Yeshayah* 59:15.

380   *Daniel* 12:10.

381   Rambam, *Selected Letters of Maimonides*, translated by Avraham Yaakov Finkel (Yeshiva Beth Moshe, 1994), pgs. 6–7.

Chapter Twenty-One

LIFE IN THE WORLD TO COME

IN A SERIES of talks given in 1948 in Gateshead, England, the great rabbi and master of Kabbalah, Rabbi Eliyahu Eliezer Dessler, presented a description of the cyclical process of *Olam Haba*, the Next World. This was translated into English from the Hebrew and entitled, "Being and Having."[382]

In order to understand life in the Next World, we must begin by examining life in this world. Life in this world is temporary, but life in the Next World is eternal. The two lives, however, are related. Like a tree growing in this world and the fruits growing in the next one, both worlds depend on each other.

He began by defining life in two ways:

- The intuition of our existence is ego-consciousness — this is the awareness of being.
- Awareness of the ego's relations with the world outside itself — this is the awareness of what we lack, both physically and spiritually, an awareness of an urge to fulfill our need, and an awareness of the actual fulfillment of the need.

This is the essence of life itself. All physical acquisitions in this world remain outside of ourselves and don't become part of our being. The

---

382　Rabbi Eliyahu Eliezer Dessler, *Strive for Truth*, trans. Aryeh Carmell (Feldheim Publishers, 1989), vol. 3, pg. 184.

houses we build and clothes we wear, the money we make and even the children we bear all reside outside of us. Even things like the feeling of honor we receive, while being enjoyable, resides in others and not intrinsically in us.

On the other hand, all spiritual acquisitions reside inside us and become part of our very being. These "acquisitions" are not merely spiritual ideas we've heard and grasped with our intellect, they are spiritual attainments that have become part of our very being to such an extent that we couldn't even imagine life without them. Let's examine an example of such an acquisition, which moves from having to being.

FROM HAVING TO BEING

Let's say you decide to work on conquering a negative character trait such as anger. You can learn quite a bit about how bad getting angry is for you. It isn't good for your health, as it leads to high blood pressure and other physical ailments. You can also see how it decreases your quality of life, as you go about your day with a feeling of anger inside of you. But by learning or reading about the negative aspects of anger, you still haven't conquered the anger itself.

However, when you learn to control your anger in real time, and you reach a point after many months or even years where your anger doesn't display itself except on rare occasions, then you have transitioned from having knowledge of how bad anger is for you to being a person who is not controlled by his anger. In short, you have moved from having knowledge of something to actually being through knowledge and hard work — a whole different state.

This is what Rabbi Dessler refers to as "spiritual acquisitions." These are spiritual attainments that have become internalized to such an extent that you could not imagine yourself without them. This is really what the World to Come is all about: changing yourself in a positive direction to such a degree that the change becomes part of your being and will accompany you to the Next World.

Physical things such as fine food, homes, money, cars, and the like are not bad. On the contrary, Jewish thought sees the entire physical world as a potential force for good. However, when it comes to physical things, you can merely "have" them; at no point do they become part of your "being." You can grasp them with your intellect, and you may be emotionally aroused to aspire to them, but they will always remain outside of you in the world of "having." After some work, the results of using the physical blessings for good will allow you to take your accomplishments until they become real within you and part of your being.

ARE YOU IN THE WORLD TO COME, OR IS THE WORLD TO COME IN YOU?

The performance of any mitzvah has the power to convert theoretical knowledge of Torah (from where we learn all the mitzvos) into a permanent reality in one's heart. So by doing a mitzvah, we have turned Torah knowledge into real being. The Torah becomes alive inside and creates permanent change. By doing this, we have allowed a part of the World to Come to enter into us without even realizing it. Later, when our souls leave our bodies at the time of death, it will become clear that all our spiritual efforts were not for naught and were actually the real acquisitions we were making through our lives.

One could summarize this idea into one neat quote: It's not that the righteous person is in the World to Come, but the exact opposite — the World to Come is in the righteous person. As one grows as a person and focuses one's attention on the real purpose of life, i.e., becoming a better person, then the move from the Present World to the Next World becomes a seamless transition.

> It's not that the righteous person is in the World to Come, but the World to Come is in the righteous person.

The Torah tells us that G-d told the Jewish people that He is "placing before [us] blessing and curse."[383] This, explains the *Daas Zekeinim*, is only in this lower world where there exists a mixture of blessing and curse; in the world after the arrival of the Mashiach, there will be only blessing.

---

383 *Devarim* 11:27.

THE KISS OF DEATH

The result of living a life of being, as opposed to merely having, is illustrated quite graphically in the Talmud. The Talmud describes the best and worst form of death for a person:[384]

- The worst is called *askera*, while the best is referred to as *neshikah*, or the Kiss of Death. The *askera* is a form of strangulation and occurs when the soul leaves the body in a state of pain. The Talmud compares it to branches of thorns that are caught in a ball of wool. In this way, the soul does not easily detach from the body.

- However, the *neshikah* is considered the best way to die and is compared to removing a hair from a glass of milk. This metaphor means that a truly spiritual person has little connection to the physical world. Even if he possesses many physical things, he doesn't attach his being to any of them, and when it comes time for his soul to leave his body, the process of divesting his bodily garb brings him happiness; it is a smooth transition, much like removing a hair from milk.

A number of righteous people from history merited a death through *neshikah*, says the Talmud, including Avraham, Yitzchak, Yaakov, Aaron, Miriam, and Moshe Rabbeinu.[385] These great individuals and those like them were of such a great spiritual level that even though they lived in this world and some of them possessed great material wealth, they were not defined by what they had but by what they became. In such a case, explain the Sages, it is G-d Himself who performs the *neshikah*, removing the soul from the body at the end of life, and not the Angel of Death.

What still needs to be examined is: What will life be like in *Olam Haba*?

---

384   *Berachos* 8a.
385   *Bava Basra* 17a.

PEOPLE WILL WANT TO DO GOOD

Part of the description of *Olam Haba* is that the desire to do evil will be drastically reduced and, according to some, banished completely. According to the Torah, Moshe Rabbeinu prophesied about this profound change occurring after the coming of the Mashiach. It says in the Torah, "Hashem your G-d will bring you to the Land that your forefathers possessed and you shall possess it. He will do good to you and make you more numerous that your forefathers. Hashem your G-d will circumcise your heart and the heart of your offspring, to love Hashem, your G-d, with all your heart and with all your soul, that you may live."[386]

This reference to "circumcision of the heart" is a metaphor describing the removal of spiritual blockages that may be holding us back from achieving spiritual success. The "foreskin" is the spiritual barrier that prevents goodness from directing our hearts. However, after the Redemption, man's natural inclination will only be to do good. So the "circumcision" of this verse is the removal from humanity of the natural desire to sin.

The Ramban explains this idea a little further. He says: "Since the dawn of Creation, man has had the free will to choose whether to be righteous or wicked, and so it was at the time of the Torah. This situation facilitated man being able to earn merit through the correct use of his free will for good or to be punished for misusing it for the bad. But in the days of the Mashiach, it will be natural to choose the good. There will be no desire for that which is not correct; people will simply not want it."[387]

The prophet Yechezkel says, "I will give you a new heart, and put a new spirit within you, and I will remove the heart of stone from your flesh, and I will give you a heart of flesh."[388] Rashi defines this "new heart" as an inclination that has been renewed for the better.

---

386 *Devarim* 30:5–6.
387 Ibid. 36:6.
388 *Yechezkel* 36:26.

PLENTIFUL WORLD

Since in the Messianic era the world will be full of all good things, and all sorts of delicacies will be common and plentiful for all people, the desire for jealousy and competition will disappear. Many wars happen between nations because they lack resources. Since during the Messianic era the world will be full of all the necessary resources, these wars will cease to exist. As society moves towards perfection and the world becomes increasingly G-dly, humanity's main preoccupation will only be to understand G-d. Yeshayah was describing this when he said, "The earth will be filled with the knowledge of Hashem as water covering the seabed."[389]

Although mankind will still have free will in the Messianic age, people will have every inducement to do the right thing and choose good. It will appear as the desire for evil will have been totally annihilated, but really people will just desire to do the right thing.

At some point during the Messianic era, the world will experience *Techi'as HaMeisim*, the Resurrection of the Dead. Let's begin to understand this very difficult yet intriguing topic.

---

389   *Yeshayah* 11:9.

Chapter Twenty-Two

THE RESURRECTION OF THE DEAD AND ITS ROLE IN THE MESSIANIC ERA

THE RAMBAM LISTED the Thirteen Principles of Faith that every Jew must know and believe in.[390] These principles are the foundation of Judaism and are the underpinnings for everything we believe as a nation. The majority of this book has been about Principle Twelve, which describes our belief in the coming of the Mashiach. However, the last in the list, Principle Thirteen, is important to understand as well, and the fact that it follows immediately after the belief in the Mashiach means that it does have some interplay and overlap with the arrival of the Mashiach.

Principle Thirteen reads: "I believe with a complete faith that there will be a resurrection of the dead whenever the Creator wills it." What is the Rambam talking about? What is this resurrection about and who is to be resurrected?

After the Messianic period comes to a close, a new and more incredible world will open up, referred to as *Olam Haba*, the Next World. This time period will begin after the Resurrection of the Dead. While the prophets spoke at great length and detail about the Messianic era, very

---

390   A full list of these principles with an explanation can be found at the end of the book in the appendix.

little was spoken about the resurrection and the nature of the world that follows it.

The Rambam writes about this and says, "A human being does not have the capacity to properly comprehend the goodness of the World to Come. No one knows its glory, beauty, and potency except for G-d himself. All the benefits that the prophets predicted for Israel are only physical matters that the Jewish people will enjoy in the Messianic era when their sovereignty is restored. The goodness of the life of the World to Come is immeasurable and utterly beyond comparison. The prophets did not describe it by means of analogy lest they cheapen it by doing so. This is just as Yeshayah HaNavi said about the World to Come, "No eye except yours, O G-d, has seen."[391]

Having said this, we are actually given a little information about this period, mostly through metaphor and analogy, so let's look at what the prophets and Sages have to say about it.

WHERE IN THE WORLD IS THE WORLD TO COME?

When a person dies, his soul goes to the *Olam HaNeshamos*, the World of Souls. This place, also referred to as *Gan Eden*, the Garden of Eden, is a non-physical and totally spiritual reality where the souls of the righteous exist in a place of profound spiritual light through their proximity to G-d. Being in a physical body for the duration of a person's life on earth, the soul never experienced such closeness to pure spirituality, as physicality acted as a barrier. However, once the body dies, the soul becomes free to experience the spiritual world in a way it never did while residing on earth. All of this takes place in the non-physical realm.

The Mashiach will come to *Olam Hazeh*, the Present World, and redeem the world, bringing the much sought-after peace we have all been waiting and praying for all these years. But what of the souls of the righteous who have passed and were not present during the Messianic Redemption? Do they not get to partake in the final part of world history? They worked as much as their descendants in laying the foundation

---

391   *Yeshayah* 64:3; Rambam, *Mishneh Torah, Teshuvah* 8:7.

for the Mashiach's arrival! Don't they get to be part of that process? The answer is yes, but not in the way you would expect.

The souls remain in the World of Souls until the final judgment that ushers in a period called *Techi'as HaMeisim*, Resurrection of the Dead, and the World to Come. Unlike the World of Souls, which is a holding station of sorts for the souls that departed this world for the duration of world history, both the Resurrection of the Dead and the World to Come will take place in this physical world after the Mashiach has revealed himself and peace has reigned over the entire world.

THE THREE PHASES OF JUDGMENT

Every person is judged, says the Ramban before the Heavenly Tribunal at three stages of their existence.[392] Let's examine each one of these three judgments in a little more detail:

1. Every Rosh Hashanah, a person's material fortunes are decided according to their deeds during the preceding year. It's on Rosh Hashanah that every soul in the world goes through this accounting and is scrutinized as to its worth and accomplishments from the previous year. Based on this accounting, the decision is made for the material success for that person during the upcoming year: how much money they will acquire, if they are to be married, how many children they will be given, and all the challenges they will need to face in order to achieve their potential.

2. At death, the soul of every person is judged and the decision is made whether they go straight to the World of Souls, or whether they go to Gehinom for a short cleansing period before they are permitted to enter the World of Souls.

3. At *Yom HaDin*, the Great Day of Judgment, all people are judged to determine whether they are worthy of resurrection. Even though every person was already judged when he died,

---

392   *Shaar HaGemul*, based on *Rosh Hashanah* 16b.

this new judgment adds another element that could not be judged when they passed, i.e., the long-term consequences of the actions from their sojourn on earth. Explains Rabbi Aharon Kotler, "As an example, Moshe's influence is felt to this very day, [so] his final judgment on the Great Day of Judgment will include his effect on subsequent generations in addition to his actions when he was living. This is true for the rest of us, as well. The final judgment takes into account the sum total of every person's accomplishment and influence up to the last day of history."[393]

WHAT IS THE RESURRECTION AND WHO GETS RESURRECTED?

At some point in the Messianic era, G-d will resurrect the dead. There are different opinions as to when this will occur:

- Some say the resurrection will occur soon after the arrival of the Mashiach;
- Others believe it will take place right at the end of the Messianic era;
- Many assert that both of these opinions are true — that the Resurrection of the Dead will occur in two stages. At the time of the Messianic Redemption, the *tzadikim gemurim*, the completely righteous, will be resurrected so that they will then be able to achieve the levels they were denied in their first lives because of the adverse conditions of this world. Later, on the Great Day of Judgment, there will be a general resurrection of all people for purpose of reward and punishment.

Daniel the Prophet states: "Many of those who sleep in the dust of the earth will awaken; these for everlasting life, these for shame and for

---

393   Rabbi Aharon Kotler, *Mishnas Rabbi Aharon* I, pg. 252.

eternal disgrace."[394] This statement, says the Talmud, is one of many verses that discusses the Resurrection of the Dead.[395] The resurrected will include all of mankind, as Abarbanel explains,[396] the righteous will be resurrected so that they might enjoy the benefits they have merited from their lives of goodness.

> The righteous will be resurrected so that they might enjoy the benefits they have merited.

The enemies of Israel, according to Abarbanel, will also be resurrected. This will happen so that they can realize the consequences of their actions and regret the folly of their false beliefs, as they will all come to acknowledge the one true belief, as seen in the words of the prophet Tzefaniah: "For then I will change the nations to speak a pure language, so that they will all proclaim the Name of Hashem to worship Him of one accord."[397]

The Rambam disagrees.[398] He writes that the resurrection will only be for the righteous people. His opinion is based upon the Talmud, which says that while the rain is for the righteous and wicked, however Resurrection of the Dead is only for the righteous.[399]

The *Shnei Luchos HaBris* explains what humanity has to look forward to:

> *When the true ingathering of the exiles takes place, at the time our righteous Mashiach appears, Creation itself will renew itself; a new "light" will emerge. At that time body and soul will be able to fuse. Also the earth itself, though purely matter, will be full of knowledge; thus together with the perfection existing "down here," the full extent of G-d's blessings from "above" will be experienced, so that body and soul may live forever.[400]*

---

394   *Daniel* 12:2.
395   *Sanhedrin* 92a.
396   Abarbanel, *Mayanei HaYeshua* 11a.
397   *Tzefaniah* 3:9.
398   Rambam, commentary to the Mishnah, *Sanhedrin*, chap. 10.
399   *Ta'anis* 7a.
400   Shelah, *Pinchas, Torah Ohr*, 2.

WHY DO WE NEED RESURRECTION IN THE FIRST PLACE?

The obvious question is why do we even need a resurrection? The following conversation between the Roman emperor Marcus Aurelius Antoninus and Rabbi Yehudah HaNasi, affectionately known as Rebbi, may shed some light on this topic.

The Talmud discusses a conversation between Antoninus and Rebbi on the topic of the Resurrection of the Dead.[401] Antoninus asked Rebbi about the final judgment, saying that surely a person's body is able to excuse its bad behavior when it was alive, and the soul can blame the body, so why is anyone judged for their bad actions?

Rebbi gave Antoninus the following parable to help explain: A king had a beautiful orchard that had delicious figs growing in it. He placed two people to guard the orchard — a cripple and a blind man. The blind man said, "Climb onto my shoulders and we can grab and eat some of the figs." When the king arrived, he saw his figs missing. When he accused the two guards of stealing the figs, each proclaimed their innocence. The blind one said, "Do I have eyes to see the figs?" The cripple said, "Do I have functioning legs to take me to the orchard?" The king realized what had happened and mounted the cripple on the back of the blind man, and judged them together.

So too, explains the Talmud, "On the day of judgment, the Holy One, Blessed Be He, brings back the soul and injects it into the body and judges them as a unit," for the sins they committed together in life.

Rebbi explains this is how the soul and body will be reunited at the time of judgment. Rashi's explanation is that G-d will summon the soul from heaven and the body from the earth and reunite them in order to judge them as a unit.

According to Rav Sa'adiah Gaon, the righteous of the Jewish nation are resurrected at the time of the Redemption so that they can witness the promised and long-awaited Redemption.[402] Not only this, the resurrection will be an incredible miracle that will greatly enhance the belief

---

401   *Sanhedrin* 91a.
402   Rav Sa'adiah Gaon, *Emunos VeDei'os* 7.

in G-d's Omnipotence. It will also permit the many people in the past generations who never saw each other to actually meet one another in the flesh. So great prophets, kings, and sages from throughout history will have the opportunity to actually meet!

In addition, all people will be able to actually see departed family, friends, and loved ones in the flesh. This will allow Jewish people from many generations of Jewish history to live together as one large nation in the Land of Israel in splendor and great honor. Furthermore, much belief and confusion about the World to Come will be answered as information about the future will be readily available from all the great people who will be alive and able to answer questions. We will have the opportunity to ask Avraham, Yitzchak, Yaakov, Moshe, Sarah, Rivka, Rachel, and Leah any questions we may have about their lives and experiences!

We'll conclude this chapter with the words of Rabbi Samson Raphael Hirsch where he says, "The true nature of all these matters is concealed from man. In lofty matters such as the World to Come and the Resurrection of the Dead and similar things, it is sufficient for us to hold fast with perfect faith to the words of the psalmist, "For You shall not abandon my soul to the grave."[403] G-d did not make a covenant with us concerning hidden matters but only what was revealed to us to heed and fulfill His Torah. He assured us that we do not require for its fulfillment knowledge of matters distant from us in the heavens or the far reaches of the sea but only what is in our mouth and heart to fulfill them."[404]

---

403 *Tehillim* 16:10.
404 Rabbi Samson Raphael Hirsch, printed in *HaMayan*, *Teves* 5715; vol. 16, 2.

PARTING WORDS

YESHAYAH HANAVI GAVE words of encouragement to those people living at the End of Days. He reassures those people who feel that the G-d of Israel has abandoned them, that G-d has forsaken His People: "Zion says, 'G-d has forsaken me, G-d has forgotten me.'" The desperate feeling of the people before the Mashiach's arrival is understandable, however Yeshayah continues, "Can a woman forget her baby, or disown the child of her womb? I never could forget you."[405]

This message is reminiscent of the words of Moshe Rabbeinu where he says, "G-d will bring back your remnants and have mercy on you. Hashem your G-d will once again gather you from among all the nations where he scattered you."[406]

These words have traveled with the Jewish people throughout our entire history. No matter how many challenges we have faced as a people — from exiles, to crusades, to pogroms to holocaust — G-d has never and will never forget us. A promise was made to our ancestors that still stands today — that a direct descendant of David HaMelech will one day come and fulfill all the words of our prophets and Sages to redeem us and bring us back to our land, Israel.

At that time, a time only known to G-d, a true peace will envelop the world, and as the prophet Yeshayah reassured us, we will see no more war or bloodshed ever again on earth. That's a true peace for all people.

May we all see the true Mashiach come to us and redeem us speedily in our days!

---

405   *Yeshayah* 49:14–15.
406   *Devarim* 30:3.

LIST OF MESSIANIC PROPHECIES

WORLD PEACE

Yeshayah 2:4

He will judge among the nations, and will settle the arguments of many peoples. They shall beat their swords into plowshares and their spears into pruning hooks; nation will not lift sword against nation and they will no longer study warfare.

Yeshayah 11:6–9

The wolf will live with the sheep and the leopard will lie down with the kid; and a calf, a lion cub and a fatling will walk together, and a young child will lead them. A cow and bear will graze and their young will lie down together; and a lion, like cattle, will eat straw. A child will play over the hole of a snake and a newly earned child will stretch his hand toward an adder's lair. They will neither injure nor destroy in all of My sacred mountain, for the earth will be filled with the knowledge of Hashem as water covering the seabed.

Michah 4:3–7

He will judge between many peoples, and will settle the arguments of mighty nations from far away. They shall beat their swords into plowshares, and their spears into pruning hooks; nations shall not lift the sword against nation; nor will they learn war anymore. They will sit, each man under his vine and under his fig tree, and none will make them afraid, for the Mouth of Hashem, Master of Legions, has spoken. For all peoples shall go, each one in the name of his god, but we will go in the name of Hashem, our G-d, forever and ever. On that day, the Word of Hashem, I will assemble the lame one, and the lost one I will gather, and those whom I harmed. And I will make the lame one into a remnant, and the scattered one into a mighty nation, and Hashem shall reign over them on Mount Zion from now and forever.

Tzefaniah 3:12–16

And I will leave over in your midst a humble people low in spirit, and they shall take shelter in the Name of Hashem. The remnant of Israel shall neither commit injustice nor speak lies; neither shall deceitful speech be found in their mouth, for they shall graze and lie down, with no one to cause them to be afraid. Sing, O daughter of Zion! Sound the trumpet, O Israel! Rejoice and jubilate wholeheartedly, O daughter of Yerushalayim! Hashem has removed your judgment; He has cast out your enemy. The king of Israel, Hashem, is in your midst, you shall no longer fear evil. On that day it shall be said to Yerushalayim, "Have no fear! O Zion, do not despair."

Zechariah 8:3–6

So said Hashem: I have returned to Zion, and I have made my dwelling in the midst of Yerushalayim; and Yerushalayim will be called the "City of Truth," and the mountain of Hashem, Master of Legions, "The Holy Mountain." So said Hashem, Master of Legions: Old men and old women will once again sit in the streets of Yerushalayim, each man with his staff in his hand because of old age. And the streets of the city shall be filled with boys and girls playing in its streets. So said Hashem, Master of Legions: As it will be wonderful in the eyes of the remnant of this people in those days, it will also be wonderful in My eyes, says Hashem, Master of Legions.

UNIVERSAL KNOWLEDGE OF G-D

Yeshayah 11:9

They will neither injure nor destroy in all of My sacred mountain, for the earth will be filled with the knowledge of Hashem as water covering the seabed.

Yirmiyah 31:33

They will no longer teach, each man his fellow, each man his brother, saying, "Know Hashem!" For they shall all know Me from their smallest to their greatest, says Hashem, for I will forgive their iniquity and I will no longer remember their sin.

Zechariah 8:20–23

So said Hashem, Master of Legions: There will yet be a time that peoples and the inhabitants of many cities shall come. And the inhabitants of one city shall go to another, saying, "Let us go to pray before Hashem and seek out Hashem, Master of Legions!" They will answer, "I, too, will go." And many peoples and powerful nations shall come to seek out Hashem in Yerushalayim, and to pray before Hashem. So said Hashem, Master of Legions, In those days, when ten men of all the languages of the nations shall take hold of the garment of a Jewish man, saying, "Let us go with you, for we have heard that G-d is with you!"

Zechariah 14:9

Hashem shall become King over all the earth; on that day Hashem will be One and His Name will be One.

Tzefaniah 3:9

For then I will change the nations to speak a pure language, so that they will all proclaim the name of Hashem to worship Him of one accord.

Michah 4:1–2

It will be in the End of Days that the mountain of the Temple of Hashem will be firmly established as the most prominent of the mountains, and it will be exalted up above the hills, and peoples will stream to it. Many nations will go and say, "Come let us go up to the mountain of Hashem and to the Temple of the G-d of Yaakov, and He will teach us of His ways and we will walk in His paths." For from Zion shall go forth the Torah, and the word of Hashem from Yerushalayim.

RESURRECTION OF THE DEAD

Yeshayah 26:19

May Your dead live, may my corpse arise; awaken and sing, you who dwell in the dust, for Your dew is like the dew that revives vegetation.

Daniel 12:2

Many of those who sleep in the dust of the earth will awaken; these for everlasting life, these for shame and for eternal disgrace.

Yechezkel 37:12–13

Therefore, prophesy and say to them, "So says the Lord Hashem/*Elokim*: Behold, I am opening your graves and raising you up from your graves as My People, and I will bring you home to the Land of Israel. Then you will know that I am the Hashem, when I open your graves and lead you up out of your graves as My People."

INGATHERING OF ISRAEL

Yeshayah 11:11–12

It shall be on that day that the Lord will once again show His hand to acquire the remnant of His people, who will have remained from Assyria and from Egypt and from Pathos and from Cush and from Elam and from Shiner and from Hamath and from the islands of the sea. He will raise a banner for the nations and He will gather the lost of Israel, and He will gather in the dispersed ones of Yehudah from the four corners of the earth.

Yeshayah 27:12–13

And it shall be on that day, that Hashem shall gather from the surging Euphrates River to the stream of Egypt, and you shall be gathered up one by one, O Children of Israel. And it shall come to pass on that day that a great *shofar* shall be sounded, and those lost in the Land of Assyria and those exiled in the Land of Egypt shall come together and they will prostrate themselves to Hashem on the holy mountain in Yerushalayim.

Yeshayah 43:5–6

Fear not for I am with you; from the East I will bring your offspring, and from the West I will gather you. I will say to the North, "Give them over!" And to the South, "Do not refrain"; bring My sons from afar and My daughters from the ends of the earth.

Yirmiyah 16:15

But rather, "As Hashem lives, Who brought up the Children of Israel from the land of the North and from all the lands where He scattered them, and I will return them to their land that I gave to their forefathers."

Yirmiyah 23:3

And I will gather together the remnant of My flocks from all the lands where I have dispersed them, and I will restore them to their dwellings and they will be fruitful and multiply.

Yechezkel 34:11–16

For so said the Lord Hashem/*Elokim*: Behold I am here, and I will seek out My sheep and I will tend them. As a shepherd tends his flock on the day he is among his separated sheep, so will I tend to My flocks, and I will rescue them from all the places where they have scattered on a cloudy and dark day. I will take them out from among the nations, and I will gather them from the lands and bring them to their Land, and I will shepherd them to the mountains of Israel, by the streams and in all the dwellings of the Land. On good pasture I will pasture them, and on the mountains of the heights of Israel will be their dwelling; there they will lie in a good fold and graze on fat pastureland upon the mountains of Israel. I will pasture My flocks and I will cause them to lie down, says the Lord Hashem/*Elokim*. I will search the lost and I will retrieve the one astray; I will bind the broken and I will strengthen the ill, and the fat and the strong I will destroy; I will tend them in justice.

Yechezkel 36:24–28

For I will take you from among the nations and gather you from all the lands, and I will bring you to your Land. And I will sprinkle clean water upon you, and you will be clean; from all your impurities and from all your abominations will I cleanse you. I will give you a new heart, and put a new spirit within you, and I will remove the heart of stone from your flesh, and I will give you a heart of flesh. I will put My spirit within you and I will make it that you will follow my decrees and you will guard My ordinances and fulfill them. Then will you dwell in the Land that I gave your fathers, and you will be a people to Me, and I will be a G-d to you.

Yechezkel 37:21–22

And say to them, So says the Lord Hashem/*Elokim*: Behold I will take the Children of Israel from among the nations where they have gone, and I will gather them from every side, and I will bring them to their land. And I will make them into one nation in the Land upon the mountains of Israel, and one king shall be to them all as a king; and they shall no longer be two nations, neither shall they be divided into two kingdoms ever again.

Yoel 4:1

For behold, in those days and in that time when I return the captivity of Yehudah and Yerushalayim.

Amos 9:15

And I will plant Israel in their own land, and they shall never again be uprooted from upon their land, that I have given them, said Hashem your G-d.

Michah 2:12

I will surely gather all of you, O Yaakov, all of you; I will surely gather the remnant of Israel; together I will place them together as sheep in a fold, as a flock within its pen shall they teem with people.

Tzefaniah 3:18–20

I have gathered together those who have mourned for the appointed time, they came from you who have carried a burden of shame for it. Behold at that time I will crush all those that afflict you. I will save the cripple and I will gather the stray one and I will make them for praise and a good name throughout the land of their shame. At that time, I will bring them, and at that time I will gather you, for I will make you into a good name and praise among all the peoples of the earth when I restore your captives before your eyes, said Hashem.

Zechariah 10:6–10

I will strengthen the House of Yehudah, and the House of Yosef I will save. And I will settle them, for I have mercy upon them. And they shall be as though I had not forsaken them, for I am the Hashem their G-d, and I will answer them. And Ephraim shall be like a mighty man, and their heart shall rejoice as if with wine. And their children shall see and rejoice; their heart shall be joyful with Hashem. I will whistle to them, and I will gather them, for I have redeemed them. And they shall multiply as they multiplied. And I will sow them among the peoples, and in the distant places they shall remember Me. And they shall live with their children and return. And I will return them from the Land of Egypt, and from Assyria I will gather them. And to the Land of Gilead and Lebanon I will bring them, and it shall not suffice for them.

THE BUILDING OF THE THIRD TEMPLE

Yeshayah 56:7

I will bring them to My holy mountain, and I will cause them to rejoice in My House of Prayer, their elevation offerings and their sacrifices will be acceptable upon My Altar, for My House will be called a House of Prayer for all peoples.

Yechezkel 37:26–28

And I will seal a covenant of peace with them, it will be an eternal covenant shall be with them; and I will establish them and I will multiply them, and I will place My Sanctuary in their midst forever. And My dwelling place shall be over them, and I will be to them for a G-d, and they will be to Me as a people. And the nations shall know that I am Hashem, Who sanctifies Israel, when My Sanctuary is in their midst forever.

Yechezkel 43:7

And He said to me, Son of man, this is the place of My throne and this is the place of My footstool where I shall dwell in the midst of the Children of Israel forever, and the House of Israel will no longer defile My Holy Name, they and their kings with their promiscuity, and with the corpses of their kings in their high places.

ELIYAHU HANAVI WELCOMES IN THE MESSIANIC AGE

Malachi 3:23–24

Behold I send you Eliyahu HaNavi before the coming of the great and awesome day of Hashem. And he will turn the hearts of the fathers back through the children, and the hearts of the children back through their fathers...

THE MASHIACH

Yeshayah 11:1–5

And a staff shall spring forth from the stock of Jesse, and a shoot shall sprout from his roots. And the spirit of Hashem will rest upon him, a spirit of wisdom and understanding, a spirit of counsel and strength, a spirit of knowledge and fear of the Hashem. And he shall be imbued by the fear of Hashem, and will not need to judge by what his eyes see, nor decide by what his ears hear. And he shall judge the poor with righteousness, and rebuke with fairness the humble of the earth. He will strike the wicked of the earth with the rod of his mouth and with the breath of his lips he shall put the wicked to death. And righteousness shall be the girdle of his loins, and faith the girdle of his loins.

Yirmiyah 23:5

Behold, days are coming, says Hashem, when I will establish a righteous shoot from David; a king will reign and prosper, and he will administer justice and righteousness in the Land.

Yechezkel 34:23–24

And I will establish over them a single shepherd and he will shepherd them. My servant David; he will tend them, and he will be for them as a shepherd. And I, Hashem, I will be a G-d to them, and My servant David will be a prince in their midst; I, Hashem, have spoken.

Yechezkel 37:24–25

And My servant David will be king over them, and there will be one shepherd for all of them, and they shall walk in My ordinances and observe My statutes and fulfill them. And they shall dwell on the Land that I have given to My servant, to Yaakov, wherein your forefathers lived; and they shall dwell upon it, they and their children and their children's children, forever; and My servant David shall be their leader forever.

THE THIRTEEN PRINCIPLES OF JEWISH FAITH ACCORDING TO THE RAMBAM

ONE OF THE clearest statements of Jewish belief is that contained in Maimonides' Thirteen Principles of Faith. They can be found in his commentary to the Mishnah, and in an abbreviated form in virtually every prayer book. They also form the basis of the well-known synagogue hymn, *Yigdal*.

In formulating these principles, the Rambam went through the entire length and breadth of Jewish literature and found those that encapsulate every major principle of Jewish belief. Let's have a brief look at these ideas, as they all have great significance in the verification and understanding of the belief in the coming of the Mashiach. Actually, number twelve itself is the obligation to believe in the eventual arrival of the Mashiach to redeem mankind.

FIRST PRINCIPLE:

I believe with perfect faith that G-d is the Creator and Ruler of all things. He alone has made, does make, and will make all things.

This principle involves belief in the existence of G-d. G-d is that Being, perfect in every possible way, Who is the ultimate Cause of all existence. This idea can be found in the Torah in the first of the

Ten Commandments, "I am the Lord your G-d."[407] G-d brought everything into existence, and all things depend upon Him — from the angels to the planets, from humans, animals, and the plants and trees. He has everything that He needs in Himself and does not need anything at all.

SECOND PRINCIPLE:

I believe with perfect faith that G-d is One. There is no unity that is in any way like His. He alone is our G-d — He was, He is, and He always will be.

The second principle involves the unity of G-d. We believe that the Cause of Everything is One. G-d is not one like a member of a pair or species. He is also not a single thing that can be divided into a number of elements. The Torah describes this when it says, "Hear O Israel, the Lord is our G-d, the Lord is One."[408] If a Jew believes in another deity other than G-d, he violates the commandment, "You shall have no other gods before Me."[409] G-d is the ultimate and unique unity that exists in the universe.

THIRD PRINCIPLE:

I believe with perfect faith that G-d does not have a body. Physical concepts do not apply to Him. Nothing whatsoever in the universe resembles Him at all.

This principle is that G-d is totally non-physical. This unity we call G-d is not a body or a physical force. We can't say that G-d moves, rests, or exists in a given place. Sometimes Scripture will describe G-d as seeing, walking, standing, or speaking. These are examples of Scripture speaking metaphorically, as the Talmud says, "G-d speaks in the language of man."[410]

---

407 *Shemos* 20:2.
408 *Devarim* 6:4.
409 *Shemos* 20:3.
410 *Berachos* 31b.

FOURTH PRINCIPLE:

I believe with perfect faith that G-d is first and last.

This principle involves the absolute eternity of G-d. Nothing else shares His eternal quality. This is discussed many times in Scripture when it says, "The eternal G-d is a refuge."[411] Even time itself is among the things created by G-d. Time depends upon motion. In order for motion to exist, we must have things that move. All things were created by G-d.

FIFTH PRINCIPLE:

I believe with perfect faith that it is only fitting to pray to G-d. One may not pray to anyone or anything else.

Here we learn that it is only G-d whom we are permitted to serve and pray to. We may not act in this way toward anything beneath Him, whether it be an angel, a star, one of the elements, or any combination of them. Much of the Torah discusses these ideas when it talks of the forbidden nature of idol worship.

SIXTH PRINCIPLE:

I believe with perfect faith that all the words of the Prophets are true.

Among human beings there exist people who have such lofty spiritual qualities that they achieve a level where their souls become prepared to receive pure spiritual wisdom. They receive a Divine message from G-d and they become prophets. Such individuals worked hard on perfecting their character and intelligence. They are not controlled by their impulses in any way, and have control over their emotions. Such people have the spiritual devotion that allows them to reach an exalted level of prophecy. Some even attended special schools for increasing prophecy. Just like you can grow in intellectual knowledge, so too are you able to increase your level of prophetic ability. Ultimately though, prophecy is a gift from G-d.

---

411 *Devarim* 33:27.

It is G-d who grants this ability to mankind. However, all prophets have one thing in common: they all see their prophecy in a dream or vision at night, or during the day in a trance. The message comes to the prophet in the form of an allegory. The interpretation of the allegory is immediately implanted in his mind, and he knows the meaning. For example, Yaakov saw a ladder with angels ascending and descending on it. This was an allegory for the four empires that would subjugate his descendants.

Not only must a prophet be very righteous in all his endeavors, before he is believed as a true prophet he must be tested a number of times by accurately predicting the future. They must predict such things as bounty and famine, war and peace. Even the needs of an individual may be revealed to a prophet. An example is when Shaul lost something, he went to the prophet who told him where it was. If even a single detail of his prediction does not come true, then we can be sure this person is a false prophet. Even the prophet Shmuel was tested, as it says, "And Shmuel grew, and G-d was with him, and all his words came true."[412]

A bad prophecy of impending doom does not need to happen. It is possible that through repentance G-d will avert His decree, and so he is still believed. If, however the prophet predicts good, then it must come to happen; if it doesn't we know he is a false prophet. This is because all good things that are predicted cannot be retracted.

SEVENTH PRINCIPLE:

I believe with perfect faith that the prophecy of Moshe Rabbeinu is absolutely true. He was the greatest prophet from all those before or after him.

This is the belief that Moshe Rabbeinu was the chief of all prophets. He was superior to all other prophets, whether they preceded him or came after him. Even the eventual Mashiach will not be as great a prophet as Moshe Rabbeinu. He attained the highest possible spiritual level a person can reach.

---

412 *Shmuel I* 3:18.

The prophecy of Moshe Rabbeinu was different to all other prophets in four ways:

1. G-d spoke to all other prophets through an intermediary. Moshe Rabbeinu didn't need any intermediary, as the Torah says, "Mouth to mouth I will speak to him."[413]

2. Every other prophet could only receive prophecy while sleeping. The prophecy came as a "dream at night,"[414] and a "vision at night."[415] If a prophecy came by day, the prophet received it while in a trance. For Moshe Rabbeinu, when a daytime prophecy came, he stood fully awake.

3. For other prophets, receiving prophecy was a traumatic experience. Their strength would fail and they would be full of dread at the experience, as Daniel said after receiving prophecy, "I became powerless, my appearance was disarrayed, and my strength deserted me...and I fell on the ground in a trance."[416] When the Torah describes the prophecy to Moshe Rabbeinu, it says, "G-d spoke to Moshe Rabbeinu face-to-face as a man speaks to his friend."[417] So the conversation between Moshe Rabbeinu and G-d was like a person who speaks to his friend.

4. Other prophets could not receive prophecy whenever they desired. It all depended on G-d's will. A prophet may have to wait days, months, or years and still not receive prophecy. Many prophets would call for musicians to play for them hoping that this would put them into the joyous mindset necessary to receive prophecy. Even then prophecy was not certain. Moshe Rabbeinu could prophesy whenever he desired. The Torah says that Moshe Rabbeinu said, "Now wait, and I will hear what G-d commands in your case."[418]

---

413   *Bamidbar* 12:8.
414   *Bereishis* 20:3.
415   *Iyov* 33:15.
416   *Daniel* 10:8.
417   *Shemos* 33:11.
418   *Bamidbar* 9:8.

EIGHTH PRINCIPLE:

I believe with perfect faith that the entire Torah now in our hands is the same one that was given to Moshe Rabbeinu.

This principle describes how the Torah given to us by Moshe Rabbeinu originated from G-d. G-d dictated the words and Moshe Rabbeinu wrote them down like a secretary taking dictation. The Torah is therefore the prophecy of Moshe Rabbeinu. Every word and letter in the Torah originated from G-d and all verses are perfectly equal in importance.

The same is true of the explanation of the Torah which was also given by G-d. Following this oral tradition, we make such things as a *succah*, *shofar*, *tzitzis*, and *tefillin* in exactly the same manner that G-d dictated to Moshe Rabbeinu. Every one of these and the rest of the mitzvos were given to Moshe Rabbeinu on Mount Sinai.

Moshe Rabbeinu wrote many copies of the entire Torah with his own hand shortly before he died. He gave a copy to each tribe and another was placed in the Ark as a testimony. The Oral Torah was not written down and was taught by Moshe Rabbeinu to his council, which was made up of the Seventy Elders. Since Yehoshua was the main disciple of Moshe Rabbeinu, he was responsible for the Oral Torah and he kept teaching it orally for as long as he lived. Then many elders received the tradition from Yehoshua.

From the time of Moshe Rabbeinu until Rabbi Yehudah HaNasi, no book existed from which the Oral Torah could be taught from. Each generation had leaders who would study the Oral Torah and would write their own notes. Rabbi Yehudah eventually took many of these notes and other commentaries on the entire Torah and compiled into a book called the Mishnah. This way, the entire Oral Torah was taught to many people and preserved for eternity.

Eventually, an explanation and discussion of the Mishnah was compiled by Rav Ashi and Ravina, called the Babylonian Talmud. They gathered all the teachings from many Sages since the time of Rabbi Yehudah explaining the depths and expounding the concepts in the Mishnah.

NINTH PRINCIPLE:

I believe with perfect faith that the Torah will not be changed, and that there will never be another Torah given by G-d.

This principle involves permanence. The Torah is G-d's permanent word, and no one else can change it. Nothing can be added or subtracted from either the written Torah or the Oral Torah, as the Torah says, "You shall not add to it, nor subtract from it."[419]

Through this, the mitzvos remain binding forever. A prophet cannot arrive and remove even one word of the Torah. If he tries, he is a false prophet, no matter what signs and predictions he creates or miracles he performs.

TENTH PRINCIPLE:

I believe with perfect faith that G-d knows all of man's deeds and thoughts.

This principle is that G-d knows all the actions of mankind. This denies the opinion of those who say, "G-d has abandoned His world, G-d does not see."[420] This is mentioned many times in the Torah, "G-d saw that the evil of man on earth was very great."[421] G-d knows all of our secrets and sees all things from beginning to end.

Even though G-d knows our thoughts and actions, humans still have complete freedom of will. This is a paradox that theologians have grappled with for millennia; if G-d knows the future, and knows whether you will be good or bad, how do you have free will to choose between good and bad? The Rambam answers and says as mortals we cannot fathom the ways of G-d, as Yeshayah HaNavi says, "My thoughts are not your thoughts, My ways are not your ways."[422] We therefore do not have the ability to understand how G-d knows all things and deeds, while still endowing mankind with free will. But He does.

---

419 *Devarim* 13:1.
420 *Yechezkel* 9:9.
421 *Bereishis* 6:5.
422 *Yeshayah* 55:8.

ELEVENTH PRINCIPLE:

I believe with perfect faith that G-d rewards those who keep His commandments, and punishes those who transgress His commandments.

This principle is that G-d rewards those who obey the commandments of the Torah and punishes those who violate the prohibitions. The greatest of all rewards is life in the World to Come, while the greatest punishment is being cut off from it. When we make mistakes and sin, G-d knows the exact punishment we need in order to help us improve our ways. Sometimes the punishment comes to our bodies, and other times through our possessions. And sometimes, even a small irritation in the form of taking the wrong coin out of our pocket may be sufficient as a punishment.

When a person repents by regretting his deeds, his repentance acts as a shield, protecting him from troubles.

TWELFTH PRINCIPLE:

I believe with perfect faith in the coming of the Mashiach. No matter how long it takes, I will await his coming day.

The main benefit of the Messianic era is that there will be no more wars. True peace will pervade the entire world. People will be able to spend their time doing good and righteous things. The implications for the Jewish people will be that we will no longer be subjugated by foreign governments and powers. Not only will there be no more racism, but anti-Semitism and all other forms of hatred will disappear from the world. The world will only know true and lasting peace. In addition, the Jewish people will return to their homeland Israel, where the Mashiach will return the royal dynasty of David HaMelech and the Third and final Temple will be built in Yerushalayim.

THIRTEENTH PRINCIPLE:

I believe with perfect faith that the dead will be brought back to life when G-d wills it to happen.

This principle discusses the Resurrection of the Dead. It is a concept that is mentioned many times in our prayers and Jewish liturgy, as well as in supplications written by the prophets and Sages. Many more references can be found in the Talmud and Midrashim.

The body and the soul will be reunited once again after they have been separated by death. This resurrection is literal and should not be understood allegorically. We are told by the prophet Daniel, "Many of those who sleep in the dust of the earth will awaken; these for everlasting life, these for shame and for eternal disgrace."[423] Ultimately, we will live again.

---

423   *Daniel* 12:2.

INDEX

ABOUT THE AUTHOR

RABBI LAWRENCE HAJIOFF is originally from London, England. He graduated with honors in political science from Manchester University and then studied Torah for many years in Israel and New York. After receiving rabbinic ordination, he was the official rabbi of Birthright Israel in Manhattan for fifteen years. Presently, Rabbi Hajioff is on the full-time faculty of Stern College for Women. His previous books include the bestsellers *Jew Got Questions* and *Will Jew Marry Me?*

Rabbi Hajioff lives in Monsey with his wife, Anita, and their five children. He can be reached via his website, www.rabbilawrence.com.

Made in the USA
Middletown, DE
17 December 2024